The tenth muse lately sprung up in America, or,
Severall poems compiled with great variety of wit
and learning, full of delight : wherein especially
is contained a compleat discourse and description
of the four elements, constitutions, ages of man,...

Anne Bradstreet

THE
TENTH MUSE

Lately fprung up in AMERICA.

OR

Severall Poems, compiled

with great variety of VVit
and Learning, full of delight.
Wherein efpecially is contained a com-
pleat difcourfe and defcription of

The Four { *Elements,*
Conftitutions,
Ages of Man,
Seafons of the Year.

Together with an Exact Epitome of
the Four Monarchies, *viz.*

The { *Affyrian,*
Perfian,
Grecian,
Roman.

Alfo a Dialogue between Old *England* and
New, concerning the late troubles.
With divers other pleafant and ferious Poems

By a Gentlewoman in thofe parts.

Printed at London for *Stephen Bowtell* at the figne of the
Bible in Popes Head-Alley. 1650

Kind Reader:

Ad I opportunity but to borrow some of the Authors wit, 'tis possible I might so trim this curious work with such quaint expressions, as that the Preface might bespeake thy further perusall; but I feare 'twil be a shame for a man that can speak so little, to be seene in the title page of this Womans Book, lest by comparing the one with the other, the Reader should passe his sentence, that it is the gift of women, not only to speak most, but to speake lest; I shall leave therefore to commend that, which with any ingenious Reader will too much commend the Author, unlesse men turne more peevish then women, to envie the excellency of the inferiour Sex. I doubt not but the Reader will quickly finde more then I can say, and the worst effect of his reading will be unbeleif, which will make him question whether it be a womans Work, and aske, Is it possible? If any doe, take this as an answer from him that dares avow it; It is the Work of a Woman, honoured, and e-

esteemed

steemed where she lives, for her gracious de-
meanour, her eminent parts, her pious con-
versation, her courteous disposition, her exact
diligence in her place, and discreet mannag-
ing of her family occasions; and more then
so, these Poems are the fruit but of some few
houres, curtailed from her sleep, and other re-
freshments. I dare adde little, lest I keepe
thee too long, if thou wilt not beleeve the
worth of these things (in their kind) when
a man sayes it, yet beleeve it from a woman
when thou seest it. This only I shall annex,
I feare the displeasure of no person in the pub-
lishing of these Poems but the Authors, without
whose knowledge, and contrary to her expe-
ctation, I have presumed to bring to publick
view what she resolved should never in such
a manner see theSun ; but I found that di-
vers had gotten some scattered papers, affe-
cted them wel, were likely to have sent forth
broken peices to the Authors prejudice, which
I thought to prevent, as well as to pleasure
those that earnestly desired the view of the
whole.   Mercu-

MErcury shew'd *Apollo*, *Bartas* Book,
Minerva this, and wisht him well to
   look,
And tell uprightly, which, did which excell;
He view'd, and view'd, and vow'd he could
   not tell.
They bid him Hemifphear his mouldy nofe,
With's crackt leering-glaffes, for it would
   pofe
The beft brains he had in's old pudding-pan,
Sex weigh'd, which beft, the Woman, or the
   Man?
He peer'd, and por'd, and glar'd, and faid for
   wore,
I'me even as wife now, as I was before :
They both 'gan laugh, and faid, it was no
   mar'l
The Auth'reffe was a right *Du Bartas* Girle.
Good footh quoth the old *Don*, tel ye me fo,
I mufe whither at length thefe Girls wil go;
It half revives my chil froft-bitten blood,
To fee a woman, once, do ought that's good;
And chode buy *Chaucers* Boots, and *Homers*
   Furrs,
Let men look to't, leaft women weare the
   Spurs.

                              N Ward.

To my deare Sister, the Author of these Poems.

THough most that know me, dare (I think) affirm
I ne're was borne to doe a Poet harm,
  Yet when I read your pleasant witty straines,
It wrought so strongly on my addle braines;
That though my verse be not so finely spun,
And so (like yours) cannot so neatly run,
Yet am I willing, with upright intent,
To shew my love without a complement
There needs no painting to that comely face,
That in its native beauty hath such grace,
What I (poore silly I) prefix therefore,
Can but doe this, make yours admir'd the more,
And if but only this, I doe attaine
Content, that my disgrace may be your gaine
    If women, I with women, may compare,
Your Works are solid, others weake as are,
Some books of Women I have heard of late,
Perused some, so witl'K, in rate,
So void of sence, and truth, as if to erre
Were only women (acting above their sphere)

And

And all to get, what (silly soules) they lack,
Esteeme to be the wisest of the pack,
Though (for your sake) to some this be permitted,
To print, yet wish I many better witted ;
Then vanity make this to be inquired,
If women are with wit, and sence inspired :
Yet when your Works shall come to publick view,
'Twill be affirm'd, 'twill be confirm'd by you :
And I, when seriously I had revolved
What you had done, I presently resolved,
Theirs was the Persons, not the Sexes failing,
And therefore did be-speak a modest vailing.
You have acutely in Eliza's ditty
Acquitted women, else I might with pitty,
Have wisht them all to womens Works to look,
And never more to meddle with their book.
What you have done, the Sun shall witnesse beare,
That for a womans Worke 'tis very rare ;
And if the Nine vouchsafe the Tenth a place,
I think they rightly may yeeld you that grace.
    But least I should exceed, and too much loves
Should too too much endear'd affect on move,
To super-adde in praises I shall cease,
Least while I please my selfe I should displease
The longing Reader, who may chance complaine,
And so requite my love with deep disdaine ;
That I your silly Servant, stand i' th' porch,
Lighting your Sun-light with my blinking torch ;
Hindring his minds content, his sweet repose,
Which your delightfull Poems doe disclose,
When once the Caskets op'ned , yet to you
Let this be added, then i'le bid adieu.

If you shall think, it will be to your shame
To be in print, then I must beare the blame :
If't be a fault, 'tis mine, 'tis shame that might
Deny so faire an infant of its right,
To looke abroad : I know your modest minde,
How you will blush, complaine, 'tis too unkinde,
To force a womans birth, provoke her paine,
Expose her Labours to the world's disdaine :
I know you'l say, you doe defie that mint,
That stampt you thus, to be a foole in print.
    'Tis true, it doth not now so neatly stand,
As if't 'twere pollisht with your owne sweet hand ;
'Tis not so richly deckt, so trimly tir'd,
Yet it is such as justly is admir'd
If it be folly, 'tis of both, or neither,
Both you and I, we'l both be fools together ;
And he that sayes, 'tis foolish (if my word
May sway) by my consent shall make the third.
I dare out face the worlds disdaine for both,
If you alone professe you are not wroth ;
Yet if you are, a womans wrath is little,
When thousands else admire you in each tittle.

                                 I W.

Upon

Upon the Author, by a
knowne Friend.

NOw I beleeve Tradition, which doth call
The Muses, Vertues, Graces, Females all;
Only they are not nine, e'eaten, nor three,
Our Authoresse proves them but one unity.
Mankind take up some blushes on the score,
Monopolize perfection no more·
In your owne Arts, confesse your selves out-done,
The Moone hath totally ecclips'd he Sun,
Not with her sable mantle muffling him,
But her bright silver makes his gold looke dim:
Just as his beams force our pale Lamps to winke,
And earthly Fires within their ashes shrinke

I cannot wonder at Apollo now,
That he with Female Lawrell crown'd his brow,
That made him witty. bid I leave to chuse,
My Verse should be a Page unto your Muse.

C. B.

ARme, arme, Soldado's arme, Horse,
    Horse, speed to your Horses,
Gentle-women, make head, they vent
    their plots in Verses;
They write of Monarchies, a most se-
    ditious word,
It signifies Oppression, Tyranny, and
    Sword:
March amain to *London*, they'l rise, for
    there they flock,
But stay a while, they seldome rise till
    ten a clock.

                                   R. 2.

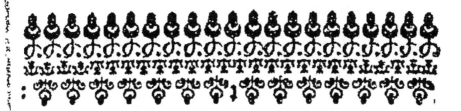

In praiſe of the Author,

Miſtris *Anne Bradſtreet*, Vertue's
tiue and lively Patterne, Wife of
the Worſhipfull *Simon* Brad-
ſtreet Eſquire.

At preſent reſiding in the Occi-
dentall parts of the World, in
America, alias

NOV-ANGLIA.

VVHat *Golden ſplendent* STAR *is*
this, ſo bright,
One thouſand miles thrice told, both day
and night,

(From

(From th' Orient first sprung) now from
   the West
That shines; swift-winged Phœbus, and
   the rest,
Of all Joves fiery flames surmounting far,
As doth each Planet, every falling Star;
By whose divine, and lucid light most cleare,
Natures darke secret Mysteries appeare;
Heaven's, Earths, admired wonders, noble
   acts
Of Kings, and Princes most herojick facts,
And what e're else in darknes seem'd to dye,
Revives all things so obvious now to th' eye;
That he who these, its glittering Rayes
   viewes o're,
Shall see what's done, in all the world before.

                   N. H.

Upon

Upon the Author.

'TWere extreame folly ſhould I dare attempt,
To praiſe this Authors worth with complement;
None but her ſelf muſt dare commend her parts,
Whoſe ſublime brain's the Synopſis of Arts:
Nature and Skil, here both in one agree;
To frame this Maſter-peice of Poetry:
Falſe Fame, belye their Sex, no more, it can,
Surpaſſe, or parallel, the beſt of man.

C. B.

Another to Mrs *Anne Bradſtreete*, Author of this Poem.

I'Ve read your Poem (Lady) and admire,
Your Sex, to ſuch a pitch ſhould e're aſpire;
Goe on to write, continue to relate,
New Hiſtories, of Monarchy and State
And what the *Romans* to their Poets gave,
Be ſure ſuch honour, and eſteem you'l have

H S.

An

An Anagram.

Anna Bradestreate.

Deer Neat *An Bartas.*

So *Bartas* like thy fine spun Poems been,
That *Bartas* name will prove an Epicene

Another.

Anne Bradstreate.

Artes bred neat *An.*

To her moſt Honoured Fa-
ther *Thomas Dudley Eſq;*
theſe humbly preſented.

DEare Sir, of late delighted with the ſight,   *T D on the*
   Of your *four ſiſters, deckt in black&white* *four parts*
Ot fairer Dames, the ſun near ſaw the face , *of the*
(though made a pedeſtall for *Adams* Race) *world*
Their worth ſo ſhines, in thoſe rich lines you ſhow.
Their paralells to find I ſcarcely know,
To climbe their Climes, I have nor ſtrength, nor skill,
To mount ſo high, requires an Eagles quill .
Yet view thereof, did cauſe my thoughts to ſoare,
My lowly pen, might wait upon thoſe four,
I bring my four , and four, now meanly clad,
To do their homage unto yours moſt glad.
Who for their age, their worth, and quality,
Might ſeem of yours to claime precedency ;
But by my humble hand thus rudely pen'd
They are your bounden handmaids to attend.
Theſe ſame are they, of whom we being have,
Theſe are of all, the life, the nurſe, the grave,
Theſe are the hot, the cold, the moiſt, the dry,
That ſinke, that ſwim, that fill, that upwards flye,

Of these confifts, our bodyes, cloathes, and food,
The world, the ufefull, hurtfull, and the good:
Sweet harmony they keep, yet jar oft times,
Their difcord may appear, by these harfh rimes.
Yours did conteft, for Wealth, for Arts, for Age,
My firft do fhew, their good, and then their rage,
My other four, do intermixed tell
Each others faults, and where themfelves excell :
How hot, and dry, contend with moift, and cold,
How Aire, and Earth, no correfpondence hold,
And yet in equall tempers, how they gree,
How divers natures, make one unity.
Some thing of all (though mean) I did intend,
But fear'd you'ld judge, one *Bartas* was my friend,
I honour him, but dare not wear his wealth,
My goods are true (though poor) I love no ftealth,
But if I did, I durft not ferd them you,
Who muft reward a theife but with his due
I fhall not need my innocence to clear,
Thefe ragged lines, will do't, when they appear
On what they are, your mild afpect I crave,
Accept my beft, my worft vouchfate a grave.

From her, that to your felfe more duty owes,
Then waters, in the boundleffe Ocean flowes.

ANNE BRADSTREET

The

THE
PROLOGUE.

1.

TO fing of Wars, of Captaines, and of Kings,
Of Cities founded, Common-wealths begun,
For my mean Pen, are too fuperiour things,
And how they all, or each, their dates have run:
Let Poets, and Hiftorians fet thefe forth,
My obfcure Verfe, fhal not fo dim their worth.

2.

But when my wondring eyes, and envious heart,
Great *Bartas* fugar'd lines doe but read o're,
Foole, *I* doe grudge, the Mufes did not part
'Twixt him and me, that over fluent ftore,
A *Bartas* can, doe what a *Bartas* wil,
But fimple I, according to my skill.

3.

From School boyes tongue, no Rhethorick we expect,
Nor yet a fweet Confort, from broken ftrings,
Nor perfect beauty, where's a maine defect,
My foolifh, broken, blemifh'd Mufe fo fings,
And this to mend, alas, no Art is able,
'Caufe Nature made it fo irreparable.

4.

Nor can I, like that fluent fweet tongu'd *Greek*
Who lifp'd at firft, fpeake afterwards more plaine
By Art, he gladly found what he did feeke,
A full requita'l of his ftriving paine.

Art

Art can doe much, but this maxime's most sure,
A weake or wounded braine admits no cure

5.

I am obnoxious to each carping tongue,
Who sayes, my hand a needle better fits,
A Poets Pen, all scorne, I should thus wrong,
For such despight they cast on female wits.
If what I doe prove well, it wo'nt advance,
They'l say its stolne, or else, it was by chance.

6

But sure the antick *Greeks* were far more milde,
Else of our Sex, why feigned they those nine,
And poesy made, *Calliope's* owne childe,
So 'mongst the rest, they plac'd the Arts divine:
But this weake knot they will full soone untye,
The *Greeks* did nought, but play the foole and lye.

7

Let *Greeks* be *Greeks*, and Women what they are,
Men have precedency, and still excell,
It is but vaine, unjustly to wage war,
Men can doe best, and Women know it well,
Preheminence in each, and all is yours,
Yet grant some small acknowledgement of ours.

8

And oh, ye high flown quils, that soare the skies,
And ever with your prey, still catch your praise,
If e're you daigne these lowly lines, your eyes
Give thou some Parsley wreath, I aske no Bayes.
This meane and unrefined stuffe of mine,
Will make your glistering gold but more to shine.

A B
The

The
Foure Elements.

Ire, Aire, Earth, and Water, did all contest
which was the strongest, noblest, & the best,
Who the most good could shew, & who most
    rage
For to declare, themselves they all ingage;
And in due order each her turne should speake,
But enmity, this amity did breake.
All would be cheife, and all scorn'd to be under,
Whence issu'd raines, and winds, lightning and thunder;
The quaking Earth did groan, the skie look't black,
The Fire, the forced Aire, in sunder crack;
The sea did threat the heavens, the heavens the earth,
All looked like a Chaos, or new birth,
Fire broyled Earth, and scorched Earth it choaked,
Both by their darings, Water so provoked,
That roaring in it came, and with its force
Soone made the combatants abate their force;
The rumbling, hissing, puffing was so great,
The worlds confusion it did seeme to threat.
But Aire at length, contention so abated,
That betwixt hot and cold, she arbitrated
The others enmity: being lesse, did cease
All stormes now laid, and they in perfect peace,
That Fire should first begin, the rest consent,
Being the most impatient Element.

        B 3   *Fire.*

Fire.

WHat is my worth (both ye) and all things know,
Where little is, I can but little show,
But what I am, let learned *Grecians* say,
What I can doe, well skill'd Mechanicks may,
The benefit all Beings, by me finde,
Come first ye Artists, and declare your minde
What toole was ever fram'd, but by my might,
O Martialist! what weapon for your fight?
To try your valour by, but it must feele
My force? your sword, your Pike, your flint and steele,
Your Cannon's bootlesse, and your powder too
Without mine ayd, alas, what can they doe?
The adverse wall's not shak'd, the Mine's not blowne,
And in despight the City keeps her owne,
But I with end Granado, or Petard,
Set ope those gates, that 'tore so strong was barr'd
Ye Husband-men, your coulter's made by me,
Your shares, your mattocks, and what e're you see,
Subdue the earth, and fit it for your graine,
That so in time it might requite your paine,
Though strong limb'd *Vulcan* forg'd it by his skill,
I made it flexible unto his will
Ye Cooks, your kitchin implements I fram'd,
Your spits, pot, jacks, what else I need not name,
Your dainty food, I wholsome make, I warme
Your shrinking limbs, which winters cold doth harme
Ye Paracelsians too, in vaine's your skil
In chymestry, unlesse I help you Stil,

And

And you Philosophers, if ere you made
A transmutation, it was through mine aide.
Ye Silver-smiths, your ure I do refine,
What mingled lay with earth, I cause to shine.
But let me leave these things, my flame aspires
To match on high with the Celestiall fires
The Sun, an Orbe of Fire was held of old,
Our Sages new, another tale have told :
But be he what they list, yet his aspect,
A burning fiery heat we find reflect,
And of the selfe same nature is with mine,
Good sister Earth, no witnesse needs but thine ;
How doth his warmth refresh thy frozen backs,
And trim thee gay, in green, after thy blacks ?
Both man and beast, rejoyce at his approach,
And birds do sing, to see his glittering Coach
And though nought but *Salamanders* live in fire ,
The Flye *Pyrausta* cal'd, all else expire.
Yet men and beasts, Astronomers can tell,
Fixed in heavenly constellations dwell,
My Planets, of both Sexes, whose degree,
Poor Heathen judg'd worthy a Dietry :
With *Orion* arm'd, attended by his dog,
The *Theban* stout *Alcides*, with his club.
The Valiant *Perseus* who *Medusa* slew,
The Horse that kil'd *Bellerophon*, then flew.
My Crabbe, my Scorpion, fishes, you may see,
The maid with ballance, wayn with horses three ;
The Ram, the Bull, the Lyon, and the Beagle ,
The Bear, the Goate, th. Raven, and the Eagle,
The Crown, the Whale, the Archer, *Bernice* Hire,
The Hidra, Dolphin, Boys, that waters bear.

Nay

Nay more then these, Rivers 'mongst stars are found,
Eridanus, where *Phaeton* was drown'd,
Their magnitude and height should I recount,
My story to a Volume would amount:
Out of a multitude, these few I 'touch,
Your wisdom out of little gathers much,
Ile here let passe, my Choler cause of warres,
And influence of divers of those starres,
When in conjunction with the sun, yet more,
Augment his heat, which was too hot before:
The Summer ripening season I do claime,
And man from thirty unto fifty frame.
Of old, when Sacrifices were divine,
I of acceptance was the holy signe.
'Mong all my wonders which I might recount,
There's none more strange then *Ætna's* sulphery mount
The choaking flames, that from *Vesuvius* flew
The over-curious second *Pliny* flew.
And with the ashes, that it sometimes shed
Apulia's jacent parts were covered,
And though I be a servant to each man;
Yet by my force, master my master can.
What famous Townes to cinders have I turn'd?
What lasting Forts my kindled wrath hath burn'd?
The stately seats of mighty Kings by me.
In confus'd heaps of ashes may ye see
Where's *Ninus* great wal'd Town, and *Troy* of old?
Carthage, and hundred more, in stories told,
Which when they could not be o're come by foes
The Army through my helpe victorious rose,
Old sacred *Zion*, I demolish'd thee;
So great *Diana's* Temple was by me

                                        And

And more then bruitish *Sodome* for her luft,
With neighbouring Townes I did confume to duft,
What fhal I fay of Lightning, and of Thunder,
Which Kings, and mighty ones, amaz'd with wonder,
Which made a *Cefar*, (*Romes*) the worlds proud head,
Foolifh *Caligula*, creep under's bed
Of Metors, *Ignis Fatuus*, and the reft,
But to leave thofe to'th' wife, I judge is beft,
The rich I oft make poore, the ftrong I maime,
Not fparing life when I can take the fame;
And in a word, the World I fhal confume,
And all therein at that great day of doome;
Not before then, fhal ceafe my raging ire,
And then, becaufe no matter mo e for fire:
Now Sifters, pray proceed, each in her courfe,
As I, impart your ufefulneffe, and force.

Earth.

THe next in place, Earth judg'd to be her due,
 Sifter, in worth I come not fhort of you;
In wealth and ufe *I* doe furpaffe you all,
And Mo her Earth, of old, men did me call,
Such was my fruitfulneffe; an Epithite
Which none ere gave, nor you could claime of right,
Among my praifes this I count not leaft,
I am th'originall of man and beaft,
To tell what fundry fruits my forfoyle yeelds,
In vine yards, orchards, gardens, and corne fields,
Their kinds, their tafts, then colours, and their fmels,
Would fo paffe time, I could fay nothing elfe,

Th-

The rich and poore, wise, foole, and every sort,
Of these so common things, can make report
To tell you of my Countries, and my regions
Soone would they passe, not hundreds, but legions,
My cities famous, rich, and populous,
Whose numbers now are growne innumerous ;
I have not time to thinke of every part,
Yet let me name my *Græcia*, 'tis my heart
For Learning, Armes, and Arts, I love it well:
But chiefly, 'cause the Muses there did dwell ,
I'le here skip o're my mountaines, reaching skies,
Whether Pyrenian, or the Alpes, both lyes
On either side the country of the *Gaules*,
Strong forts from *Spanish* and *Italian* braules,
And huge great *Taurus*, longer then the rest,
Dividing great *Armenia* from the least,
And *Hemus*, whose steep sides, none foote upon,
But farewell all, for deare mount *Helicon*,
And wonderous high *Olimpus*, of such fame,
That heaven it selfe was oft call'd by that name ;
Sweet *Parnassus*, I dote too much on thee,
Unlesse thou prove a better friend to me ,
But ile skip o're these Hills, not touch a Dale,
Nor yet expatiate, in Temple vale ,
Ile here let goe, my Lions of *Numedia*,
My Panthers, and my Leopards of *Libia*,
The Behemoth, and rare found Unicorne,
Poysons sure antidote lyes in his horne.
And my Hyæna (imitates mans voyce)
Out of huge numbers, I might pick my choyce,
Thousands in woods, and planes, both wild, and tame,
But here, or there, I list now none to name ,

No,

No, though the fawning dog did urge me sore
In his behalfe to speak a word the more,
Whose trust, and valour I might here commend ;
But time's too short, and precious so to spend
But hark, ye worthy Merchants who for prize
Send forth your well man'd ships, where sun doth rise,
After three years, when men and meat is spent,
My rich commodities payes double rent
Ye *Galenists*, my Drugs that come from thence
Doe cure your patients, fill your purse with pence,
Besides the use you have, of Herbs and Plants,
That with lesse cost, neare home, supplyes your wants,
But Marriners, where got you ships and sailes ?
And Oares to row, when both my sisters failes ?
Your Tackling, Anchor, Compasse too, is mine ,
Which guides, when Sun, nor Moon, nor Stars do shine.
Ye mighty Kings, who for your lasting fames
Built Cities, Monuments call'd by your names ,
Was those compiled heapes of missy stones ?
That your ambition laid, ought but my bones ?
Ye greedy misers who do dig for gold ,
For gemmes, for silver, treasures which I hold :
Will not my goodly face, your rage suffice ?
But you will see what in my bowels lyes ?
And ye Artificers, all trades and sorts,
My bounty calls you forth to make reports,
If ought you have to use, to wear, to eate ?
But what I freely yeeld upon your sweat ?
And cholerick sister, thou (for all thine ire)
Well knowest, my fuell must maintain thy fire.
As I ingenuously (with thanks) confesse
My cold, thy (fruitfull) heat, doth crave no lesse:

But

But how my cold, dry temper, works upon
The melancholy constitution.
How the Autumnal season I do sway,
And how I force the grey head to obey.
I should here make a short, yet true narration,
But that thy method is my imitation.
Now might I shew my adverse quality,
And how I oft work mans mortality.
He sometimes findes, maugre his toyling paine,
Thistles and thornes, where he expected graine,
My sap, to plants and trees, I must not grant,
The Vine, the Olive, and the Figtree want:
The Corne, and Hay, both fall before they'r mowne;
And buds from fruitfull trees, before they'r blowne.
Then dearth prevailes, that Nature to suffice,
The tender mother on her Infant flyes.
The Husband knowes no Wife, nor father sons;
But to all outrages their hunger runnes
Dreadfull examples, soon I might produce,
But to such auditours 'twere of no use.
Again, when Delvers dare in hope of gold,
To ope those veines of Mine, audacious bold
While they thus in my intrails seem to dive,
Before they know, they are inter'd alive
Ye affrighted wighs, appal'd how do you shake
If once you feele me your foundation, quake,
Because in the abysse of my darke wombe:
Your Cities and your selves I oft intombe:
O dreadfull sepulcher! that this is true,
Korah and all his Company well knew.
And since, sure *Ital'y* full sadly knowes
What she hath lost by these my dreadfull woes.

And

And *Rome*, her *Curtius*, can't forget I think,
Who bravely rode into my 'yawning chinke.
Again, what veines of poyson in me lye ;
As *Stibium* and unfixt *Mercury*:
With divers moe, nay, into plants it creeps ;
In hot, and cold, and some benums with sleeps,
Thus I occasion death to man and beast,
When they seek food, and harme mistrust the least.
Much might I say, of the *Arabian* sands ;
Which rise like mighty billowes on the lands :
Wherein whole Armies I have overthrown,
But windy sister, 'twas when you have blown.
Ile say no more, yet this thing adde I must,
Remember sonnes, your mould is of my dust,
And after death, whether inter'd, or burn'd;
As earth at first, so into earth return'd.

Water.

SCarce Earth had done, but th' angry waters mov'd,
Sister (quoth she) it had full well behov'd
Among your boastings to have praised me;
Cause of your fruitfulnesse, as you shall see ·
This your neglect, shewes your ingratitude,
And how your subtilty would men delude.
Not one of us, all knowes, that's like to thee,
Ever in craving, from the other three :
But thou art bound to me, above the rest;
Which in thy drink, thy blood, thy sap, and best.
If I withhold, what art thou, dead, dry lump
Thou bear'st no grasse, nor plant, nor tree, nor stump

Thy extream thirst is moistened by my love,
With springs below, and showers from above;
Or else thy sun-burnt face, and gaping chipps,
Complaines to th'heaven, when I withhold my drops
Thy Bear, thy Tyger, and thy Lyon stout,
When I am gone, their fiercenesse none need doubt,
The Camell hath no strength, thy Bull no force,
Nor mettl's found in the couragious Horse.
Hindes leave their Calves, the Elephant the Fens,
The Woolves and savage Beasts, forsake their Dens.
The lofty Eagle and the Storke flye low,
The Peacock, and the Ostrich, share in woe:
The Pine, the Cedars, yea and *Daph'nes* tree,
Do cease to flourish in this misery.
Man wants his bread, and wine, and pleasant fruits,
He knowes such sweets, lyes not in earths dry roots,
Then seeks me out, in River and in Well;
His deadly mallady, I might expell.
If I supply, his heart and veines rejoyce,
If not, soon ends his life, as did his voyce.
That this is true, earth thou canst not deny,
I call thine *Egypt*, this to verifie;
Which by my fatting Nile, doth yeeld such store;
That she can spare, when Nations round are poore.
When I run low, and not o'reflow her brinks,
To meet with want, each woefull man bethinks.
But such I am, in Rivers, showers and springs,
But what's the wealth that my rich Ocean brings?
Fishes so numberlesse I there do hold,
Shouldst thou but buy, it wou'd exhaust thy gold.
There lives the oyly Whale, whom all men know,
Such wealth, but not such like, Earth thou mayst show

Th

The Dolphin (loving musique) *Arions* friend.
The crafty Barbell, whose wit doth her commend,
With thousands moe, which now I list not name,
Thy silence of thy beasts, doth cause the same.
My pearles that dangle at thy darlings ears ;
Not thou, but shell fish yeelds, as *Pliny* clears.
Was ever gem so rich found in thy trunke ?
As *Agypts* wanton *Cleopatra* drunke.
Or hast thou any colour can come nigh ;
The *Roman* Purple, double *Tirian* dye
Which *Cæsars, Consuls, Tribunes* all adorne ;
For it, to search my waves, they thought no scorne.
Thy gallant rich perfuming Amber-greece:
I lightly cast a shoare as froathy fleece.
With rowling graines of purest massy gold
Which *Spaines Americans*, do gladly hold.
Earth, thou hast not more Countrys, Vales and Mounds,
Then I have Fountaines, Rivers, Lakes and Ponds:
My sundry Seas, Black, VVhite, and Adriatique
Ionian, Baltick, and the vast *Atlantique* ,
The *Pontike, Caspian,* Golden Rivers fine
Asphaltis Lake, where nought remains alive.
But I should go beyond thee in thy boasts,
If I should shew, more Seas, then thou hast Coasts.
But note this maxime in Philosophy :
Then Seas are deep, Mountains are never high.
To speake of kinds of VVaters I'le neglect,
My divers Fountaines and their strange effect ;
My wholesome Bathes, together with their cures.
My water *Syrens,* with their guilefull lures:
Th' uncertain cause, of certain ebbs and flowes,
VVhich wondring *Aristotles* wit, ne'r knowes.

Nor will I fpeake of waters made by Art,
Which can to life, reftore a fainting heart:
Nor fruitfull dewes, nor drops from weeping eyes;
VVhich pitt, moves, and oft deceives the wife.
Nor yet of Salt, and Sugar, fweet and fmart,
Both when we lift, to water we convert
Alas, thy fhips and oares could do no good
Did they but want my Ocean, and my Flood.
The wary Merchant, on his weary beaft
Transfers his goods, from North and South and Eaft,
Unleffe I cafe his toyle, and doe tranfport,
The wealthy fraught, unto his wifhed Port.
Thefe be my benefits which may fuffice:
I now muft fhew what force there in me lyes.
The flegmy conftitution I uphold,
All humours, Tumours, that are bred of cold.
O're childehood, and Winter, I bear the fway,
Yet *Luna* for my Regent I obey
As I with fhowers oft time refrefh the earth,
So oft in my exceffe, I caufe a dearth
And with aboundant wet, fo coole the ground,
By adding cold to cold, no fruit proves found,
The Farmer, and the Plowman both complain
Of rotten fheep, lean kine, and mildew'd grain.
And with my wafting floods, and roaring torrent,
Their Cattle, Hay, and Corne, I fweep down current,
Nay many times, my Ocean breaks his bounds,
And with aftonifhment, the world confounds
And fwallowes Countryes up, ne're feen againe
And that an Ifland makes, which once was maine
Thus *Albion* (tis thought) was cut from *France*,
Cicelie from *Italy*, by th'like chance.

And but one land was *Affrica* and *Spayne*,
Untill straight *Gibralter*, did make them twaine;
Some say I swallowed up (sure 'tis a notion)
A mighty Country ith' *Atlanticke* Ocean.
I need not say much of my Haile and Snow,
My Ice and extream cold, which all men know.
VVhereof the first, so ominous I rain'd,
That *Israels* enemies, therewith was brain'd.
And of my chilling colds, such plenty be;
That *Caucasus* high mounts, are seldom free.
Mine Ice doth glaze *Europs* big'st Rivers o're,
Till Sun release, their ships can saile no more.
All know, what innundations I have made;
VVhere'n not men, but mountaines seem'd to wade
As when *Achaia*, all under water stood,
That in two hundred year, it ne'r prov'd good.
Ducalions great deluge, with many moe ;
But these are trifles to the Flood of *Noe*.
Then wholly perish'd, earths ignoble race,
And to this day, impaires her beautious face.
That after times, shall never feel like woe :
Her confirm'd sonnes, behold my colour'd bow.
Much might I say of wracks, but that Ile spare,
And now give place unto our sister Aire.

Aire.

COntent (quoth Aire) to speake the last of you,
   Though not through ignorance, first was my due,
I doe suppose, you'l yeeld without controle;
I am the breath of every living soul.

C   Mrr-

Mortalls, what one of you, that loves not me,
Aboundintly more then my fifters three?
And though you love Fire, Earth, and VVater wel;
Yet Aire, beyond all thefe ye know t'excell
I aske the man condemn'd, that's near his death
How gladly fhould his gold purchafe his breath,
And all the wealth, that ever earth did give,
How freely fhould it go, fo he might live
No world, thy witching trafh, were all but vain.
If my pure Aire, my fonnes did not fuftain
The famifht, thirfty man, that craves fupply
His moveing reafon is, give leaft I dye.
So loath he is to go, though nature's fpent,
To bid adue, to his dear Element.
Nay, what are words, which doe reveale the mind?
Speak, who, or what they will, they are but wind
Your Drums, your Trumpets, and your Organs found,
VVhat is't but forced Aire which muft rebound,
And fuch are Ecchoes, and report o th gun
VVhich tells afar, th' exployt which he huth done
Your fongs and pleafant tunes, they are the fame,
And fo's the notes which Nightingales do frame.
Ye forging Smiths, if Bellowes once were gone;
Your red hot work, more coldly would go on.
Ye Mariners, tis I that fill your Sailes,
And fpeed you to your Port, with wifhed gales.
VVhen burning heat, do b caufe you faint, I coole,
And when I fmile, your Ocean's like a Poole.
I rip the corne, I turne the grinding mill,
And with my felfe, I every vacuum fill
The ruddy fweet fanguine, is like to Aire,
And youth, and fpring, fages to me compare

My moist hot nature, is so purely thinne,
No place so subtilly made, but I get in.
I grow more pure and pure, as I mount higher,
And when I'm throughly rarifi'd, turn fire.
So when I am condens'd, I turne to water;
VVhich may be done, by holding down my vapour.
Thus I another body can assume,
And in a trice, my own nature resume
Some for this cause (of late) have been so bold,
Me for no Element, longer to hold.
Let such suspend their thoughts, and silent be;
For all Philosophers make one of me
And what those Sages, did, or spake, or writ,
Is more authentick then their moderne wit
Next, of my Fowles such multitudes there are,
Earths Beasts, and VVaters Fish, scarce can compare.
The Ostrich with her plumes, th'Eagle with her eyne;
The Phænix too (if any be) are mine;
The Stork, the Crane, the Partrich, and the Phesant,
The Pye, the Jay, the Larke, a prey to th' Peasant.
VVith thousands moe, which now I may omit,
VVithout impeachment, to my tale or wit
As my fresh Aire preserves, all things in life,
So when 'ts corrupt, mortality is rife
Then Feavors, Purples, Pox, and Pestilence,
VVith divers moe, worke deadly consequence
VVhereof such multitudes have dy'd and sied,
The living, scarce had power, to bury dead.
Yea so contagious, Countries have me known;
That birds have not scap'd death, as they have flown,
Of murrain, Cattle numberlesse did fall.
Men fear'd destruction epidemicall

C 2   Then

Then of my tempests, felt at Sea and Land,
Which neither ships nor houses could withstand.
What woeful wracks I've made, may wel appear,
If nought was known, but that before *Algire*
Where famous *Charles* the fift, more losse sustain'd,
Then in his long hot wars, which *Millain* gain'd.
How many rich fraught vessells, have I split?
Some upon sands, some upon rocks have hit
Some have I forc'd, to gaine an unknown shoare;
Some overwelm'd with waves, and seen no more.
Again, what tempests, and what hericanoes
Knowes Western Isles, *Christophers*, *Barbadoes*,
Where neither houses, trees, nor plants, I spare,
But some fall down, and some flye up with aire.
Earth-quaks so hurtful and so fear'd of all,
Imprisoned I, am the original
Then what prodigious sights, sometimes I show:
As battells pitcht ith' Aire (as Countries know,)
Their joyning, fighting, forcing, and retreat,
That earth appeares in heaven, oh wonder great!
Sometimes strange flaming swords, and blazing stars,
Portentious signes, of Famines, Plagues and Wars.
Which makes the mighty Monarchs fear their Fates,
By death, or great mutations of their States.
I have said lesse, then did my sisters three,
But what's their worth, or force, but more's in me.
To adde to all I've said, was my intent,
But dare not go, beyond my Element.

Of the foure Humours in Mans constitution.

He former foure, now ending their Dif-
course,
Ceasing to vaunt, their good, or threat their
force.
Loe other foure ſtep up, crave leave to ſhew
The native qualities, that from each flow,
But firſt they wiſely ſhew d their high deſcent,
Each eldeſt Daughter to each Element,
Choler was own'd by Fire, and Blood by Aire,
Earth knew her black ſwarth childe, Water her faire;
All having made obeyſance to each Mother,
Had leave to ſpeake, ſucceeding one the other;
But 'mongſt themſelves they were at variance,
Which of the foure ſhould have predominance,
Choler hotly claim'd, right by her mother,
Who had precedency of all the other.
But Sanguine did diſdaine, what ſhe requir'd,
Pleading her ſelfe, was moſt of all deſir'd,
Proud Melancholy, more envious then the reſt,
The ſecond, third, or laſt could not digeſt;
She was the ſilenceſt of all the ſoure,
Her wiſedome ſpake not much, but thought the more

C 3   Cold

Cold flegme, did not contest for highest place,
Only she crav'd, to have a vacant space.
Wel, thus they parle, and chide, but to be briefe,
Or wil they nil they, Choler wil be cheife,
They seeing her imperiosity,
At present yeelded, to necessity.

Choler.

TO shew my great descent, and pedigree,
Your selves would judge, but vain prolixity.
It is acknowledged, from whence I came,
It shal suffice, to tel you what I am:
My self, and Mother, one as you shal see,
But she in greater, I in lesse degree,
We both once Masculines, the world doth know,
Now Feminines (a while) for love we owe
Unto your Sister-hood, which makes us tender
Our noble selves, in a lesse noble Gender
Though under fire, we comprehend all heat,
Yet man for Choler, is the proper seat.
I in his heart erect my regal throne,
Where Monarch-like I play, and sway alone.
Yet many times, unto my great disgrace,
One of your selves are my compeers, in place:
Where if your rule once grow predominant,
The man proves boyish, sottish, ignorant,
But if ye yeeld sub-servient unto me,
I make a man, a man in highest degree,
Be he a Souldier, I more fence his heart
Then Iron Corslet, gainst a sword or dart,

Wh

What makes him face his foe, without appal?
To ſtorme a Breach, or ſcale a City wal?
In dangers to account himſelf more ſure,
Then timerous Hares, whom Caſtles doe immure?
Have ye not heard of Worthies, Demi-gods?
Twixt them and others, what iſt makes the odds
But valour, whence comes that? from none of you,
Nay milk-ſops, at ſuch brunts you look but blew,
Here's Siſter Ruddy, worth the other two,
That much wil talk, but little dares ſhe do,
Unleſſe to court, and claw, and dice, and drink.
And there ſhe wil out-bid us all, I think,
She loves a Fiddle, better then a Drum,
A Chamber wel, in field ſhe dares not come,
She'l ride a Horſe as bravely, as the beſt,
And break a ſtaffe, provided t be in jeſt,
But ſhuns to look on wounds, and bloud that's ſpilt,
She loves her ſword, only becauſe its gilt,
Then here's our ſad black Siſter, worſe then you,
She'l neither ſay, ſhe wil, nor wil ſhe doe:
But peeviſh, Male-content, muſing ſhe ſits,
And by miſpriſions, like to looſe her wits,
If great perſwaſions, cauſe her meet her foe;
in her dul reſolution, ſhe's ſlow
To march her pace, to ſome is greater pain,
Then by a quick encounter, to be ſlaine,
But be ſhe beaten, ſhe'l not run away,
She'l firſt adviſe, if't be not beſt to ſtay.
But let's give, cold, white, Siſter Flegme her right,
So loving unto all, ſhe ſcornes to fight.
If any threaten her, ſhe l in a trice,
Convert from water, to conjealed Ice;

          C 2   Her

Her teeth wil chatter, dead and wan's her face,
And 'fore she be assaulted, quits the place,
She dare, not challenge if I speake amisse,
Nor hath she wit, or heat, to blush at this
Here's three of you, all sees now what you are,
Then yeeld to me, preheminence in War.
Again, who fits, for learning, science, Arts?
Who rarifies the intellectuall parts?
Whence flow fine spirits, and witty notions?
Not from our dul slow Sisters motions.
Nor sister Sanguine, from thy moderate heat,
Poor spirits the Liver breeds, which is thy feat,
What comes from thence, my heat refines the same,
And through the arteries sends o're the frame,
The vitall spirits they're call'd, and wel they may,
For when they faile, man turnes unto his clay
The Animal I claime, as wel as these,
The nerves should I not warm, soon would they freeze
But Flegme her self, is now provok'd at this,
She thinks I never shot so farre amisse,
The Brain she challenges, the Head's her feat,
But know'ts a foolish brain, that wanteth heat,
My absence proves, it plain, her wit then flyes
Out at her nose, or melteth at her eyes,
Oh, who would misse this influence of thine,
To be distill'd a drop on every line!
No, no, thou hast no spirits, thy company
Wil feed a Dropsie, or a Timpany,
The Palsie, Gout, or Cramp, or some such dolor,
Thou wast not made for Souldier, or for Schollar;
Of greasie paunch, and palled cheeks, go vaunt,
But a good head from these are distant,

But Melancholy, wouldſt have this glory thine ?
Thou ſayſt, thy wits are ſtai'd, ſubtle and fine:
Tis true, when I am midwife to thy birth,
Thy ſelt's as dul, as is thy mother Earth.
Thou canſt not claime, the Liver, Head nor Heart;
Yet haſt thy ſeat aſſign'd, a goodly part,
The ſinke of all us three, the hatefull ſpleen,
Of that black region, Nature made thee Queen ;
Where paine and ſore obſtructions,thou doſt work ;
Where envy, malice, thy companions lurke.
If once theu'rt great. what followes thereupon ?
But bodies waſting, and deſtruction.
So baſe thou art, that baſer cannot be ,
The excrement, aduſtion of me.
But I am weary to dilate thy ſhame ;
Nor is't my pleaſure, thus to blur thy name:
Onely to raiſe my honours to the Skyes,
As objects beſt appear, by contraries.
Thus arms, and arts I claim, and higher things;
The Princely quality, befitting Kings.
Whoſe Serene heads, I line with policies,
They're held for Oracles, they are ſo wiſe.
Their wrathfull looks are death, their words are laws;
Their courage, friend,and foe, and ſubject awes,
But one of you would make a worthy King :
Like our ſixt *Henry*, that ſame worthy thing.
That when a Varlet, ſtruck him o're the ſide,
Forſooth you are to blame, he grave reply'd.
Take choler from a Prince, what is he more,
Then a dead Lyon? by beaſts triumpht ore.
Again,ye know,how I act every part
By th' influence I ſend ſtill from the heart.

Its not your muscles, nerves, nor this nor that :
Without my lively heat, do's ought thats flat.
The spongy Lungs, I feed with frothy blood,
They coole my heat, and so repay my good.
Nay, th' stomach, magazeen to all the rest,
Without my boiling heat cannot digest,
And yet to make, my greatnesse far more great·
What differences the Sex, but only heat ?
And one thing more to close with my narration.
Of all that lives, I cause the propagation
I have been sparing, what I might have said,
I love no boasting, that's but childrens trade·
To what you now shal say, I wil attend,
And to your weaknesse, gently condescend .

Blood.

GOod sisters give me leave (as is my place)
To vent my griefe, and wipe off my disgrace
Your selves may plead, your wrongs are no whit lesse,
Your patience more then mine, I must confesse
Did ever sober tongue, such language speak?
Or honestie such ties, unfriendly break ?
Do'st know thy selfe so well, us so amisse ?
Is't ignorance, or folly causeth this ?
Ile only shew the wrongs, thou'st done to me.
Then let my sisters, right their injury .
To pay with railings, is not mine intent,
But to evince the truth, by argument
I will annalise, thy so proud relation;
So ful of boasting, and prevarication

Thy

Thy childish incongruities, Ile show :
So walke thee til thou'rt cold, then let thee go.
There is no Souldier, but thy selfe thou say st,
No valour upon earth, but what thou hast.
Thy foolish provocations, I despise.
And leave't to all, to judge where valour lyes.
No pattern, nor no Patron will I bring,
But *David*, *Judah*'s most heroyick King:
Whose glorious deeds in armes, the world can tel,
A rosie cheek'd musitian, thou know'st wel.
He knew *how*, for to handle, Sword and Harpe,
And how to strike ful sweet, as wel as sharpe.
Thou laugh st at me, for loving merriment:
And scorn'st all Knightly sports, at turnament
Thou sayst. I love my sword, because tis guilt.
But know, I love the blade, more then the hilt.
Yet do abhorre, such timerarious deeds,
As thy unbridlea, barb'rous Choler yeelds.
Thy rudenesse counts, good manners vanity,
And real complements, base flattery
For drink, which of us twain, like it the best,
Ile go no further then thy nose for test
Thy other scoffes not worthy of reply,
Shal vanish as of no validity.
Of thy black calumnies, this is but part,
But now Ile shew, what Souldier thou art.
And though thou st ut'd me, with opprobrious spight,
My ingenuity must give thee right
Thy Choler is but rage, when tis most pure.
But useful, when a mixture can indure
As with thy mother Fire, so tis with thee,
The best of al the four, when they agree.

But

But let her leave the rest, and I presume,
Both them and all things else, she will consume,
Whil'st us, for thine associates thou takest,
A Souldier most compleat in al points makest
But when thou scorn'st to take the helpe we lend,
Thou art a fury, or infernal Fiend
Witnesse the execrable deeds thou'st done
Nor sparing Sex, nor age, nor fire, nor son.
To satisfie thy pride, and cruelty
Thou oft hast broke bounds of humanity.
Nay should I tel, thou wouldst count me no blab,
How often for the lye, thou'st giv'n the stab
To take the wal's a sin, of such high rate,
That naught but blood, the same may expiate
To crosse thy wil, a challenge doth deserve
So spils that life, thou'rt bounden to preserve.
Wilt thou this valour, manhood, courage cal
Nay; know 'tis pride, most diabolical
If murthers be thy glory, t's no lesse.
Ile not envy thy feats, nor happinesse.
But if in fitting tim, and place, on foes,
For Countries good, thy life thou darst expose:
Be dangers neer so high, and courage great,
Ile praise that fury, valour, choler, heat.
But such thou never art, when al alone;
Yet such, when we at four are joyn'd in one.
And when such thou art, even such are we,
The friendly coadjutors, stil to thee
Nextly, the spirits thou do'st wholly claime,
Which natural, vital, animal we name.
To play Philosopher, I have no list,
Nor yet Phisitian, nor Anatomist

For acting theſe, I have nor wil, nor art,
Yet ſhal with equity give thee thy part,
For th' natural, thou doſt not much conteſt,
For there are none, thou ſay'ſt, if ſome, not beſt.
That there are ſome, and beſt, I dare averre,
More uſeful then the reſt, don't reaſon erre ;
What is there living, which cannot derive
His life now animal, from vegative ?
If thou giv'ſt life, I give thee nouriſhment,
Thine without mine, is not, 'tis evident.
But I, without thy help can give a growth,
As plants, trees, and ſmall Embryon know'th,
And if vital ſpirits do flow from thee,
I am as ſure, the natural from me,
But thine the nobler, which I grant, yet mine
Shal juſtly claime priority of thine .
I am the Fountaine which thy Ciſterns fils,
Through th' warme, blew conduits of my venal rils ;
What hath the heart, but what's ſent from the liver ?
If thou'rt the taker, I muſt be the giver .
Then never boaſt of what thou do'ſt receive,
For of ſuch glory I ſhal thee bereave ,
But why the heart, ſhould be uſurpt by thee,
I muſt confeſſe, is ſomewhat ſtrange to me,
The ſpirits through thy heat, are made perfect there,
But the materials none of thine, that's cleare,
Their wondrous mixture, is of blood, and ayre,
The firſt my ſelf, ſecond my ſiſter faire,
But i'le not force retorts, nor do thee wrong,
Thy fiery yellow froth, is mixt among.
Challenge not all, 'cauſe part we do allow,
Thou kno's't I'ye there to do, as wel as thou,

But

But thou wilt say, I deale unequally,
There lives the irascible faculty:
Which without all dispute, is Cholers owne ;
Besides the vehement heat, only there known,
Can be imputed unto none, but Fire ,
Which is thy self, thy *Mother*, and thy Sire ;
That this is true, I easily can assent,
If stil thou take along my Aliment,
And let me be thy Partner, which is due,
So wil I give the dignity to you
Again, stomacks concoction thou dost claime,
But by what right, nor do'st, nor canst thou name ;
It is her own heat, not thy faculty,
Thou do'st unjustly claime, her property,
The help she needs, the loving Liver lends,
Who th'benefit o'th' whole ever intends :
To meddle further, I shal be but shent,
Th'rest to our Sisters, is more pertinent
Your slanders thus refuted, takes no place,
Though cast upon my guiltlesse blushing face ;
Now through your leaves, some little time i'le spend ,
My worth in humble manner, to commend.
This hot, moist, nurtritive humour of mine,
When 'tis untaint, pure and most genuine
Shal firstly take her place, as is her due,
Without the least indignity to you ;
Of all your qualities I do partake,
And what you singly are, the whole I make.
Your hot, dry, moyst, cold, natures are foure,
I moderately am all, what need I more :
As thus, if hot, then dry ; if moist, then cold ;
If this can't be disprov'd, then all I hold .

My

My vertues hid, i've let you dimly see;
My sweet complexion, proves the verity,
This scarlet die's a badge of what's within,
One touch thereof so beautifies the skin;
Nay, could I be from all your tangs but pure,
Mans life to boundlesse time might stil endure;
But here's one thrusts her heat, where'ts not requir'd
So suddenly, the body all is fir'd.
And of the sweet, calme temper, quite bereft,
Which makes the mansion, by the soul soon left;
So Melancholly ceases on a man,
With her uncheerful visage, swarth and wan;
The body dryes, the mind sublime doth smother,
And turns him to the wombe of 's earthy mother,
And Flegm. likewise can shew, her cruel art,
With cold distempers, to pain every part;
The Lungs, the rots, the body weares away,
As if she'd leave no flesh to turn to clay,
Her languishing diseases, though not quick,
At length demolishes the faberick,
All to prevent, this curious care I take,
Ith' last concoction, segregation make.
Of all the perverse humours from mine owne,
The bitter choler, most malignant knowne
I turn into his cel, close by my side,
The Melancholly to the Spleen to 'bide;
Likewise the Whey, some use I in the veines,
The over plas I send unto the reines,
But yet for all my toyl, my care, my skil,
It's doom'd by an irrevocable wil:
That my intents should meet with interruption,
This mortal man, might turn to his corruption.

I

I might here shew, the noblenesse of minde,
Of such as to the Sanguine are inclin'd,
They're liberal, pleasant, kinde, and courteous,
And like the Liver, all benignious,
For Arts, and Sciences, they are the fittest,
And maugre (Choler) stil they are the wittest,
An ingenious working phantasie,
A most volumnious large memory,
And nothing wanting but solidity.
But why, alas, thus tedious should I be?
Thousand examples, you may daily see
If time I have transgrest, and been too long,
Yet could not be more breif, without much wrong.
I've scarce wip'd off the spots, proud Choler cast,
Such venome lyes in words, though but a blast,
No braggs i've us'd, t'your selves I dare appeale,
If modesty my worth do not conceale
I've us'd no bitternesse, nor taxt your name,
As I to you, to me, do ye the same.

Melancholy.

HE that with two assaylents hath to do,
Had need be armed wel, and active too,
    Especially when freindship is pretended.
That blow's most deadly, where it is intended,
Though Choler rage, and rule, i'le not do so,
The tongue's no weapon to assault a foe,
    sith we fight with words, we might be kind,
To spare our selves, and beat the whistling winde.

Fure

Faire roſie Siſter, ſo might'ſt thou ſcape free,
I le flatter for a time, as thou did'ſt me,
But when the firſt offenders I have laid,
Thy ſoothing girds ſhal fully be repaid,
But Choler, be thou cool'd, or chaf'd, i'le venter,
And in contentions liſts, now juſtly enter.
Thy boaſted valour ſtoutly's been repell'd,
If not as yet, by me, thou ſhalt be quell'd:
What mov'd thee thus to villiſie my name?
Not paſt all reaſon, but in truth all ſhame·
Thy fiery ſpirit ſhal bear away this prize,
To play ſuch furious pranks I am too wiſe;
If in a Souldier raſhneſſe be ſo precious,
Know, in a General its moſt perricious.
Nature doth teach, to ſheild the head from harm,
The blow that's aim'd thereat is latch'd by th'arm,
When in Battalia my foes I face,
I then command, proud Choler ſtand thy place,
To uſe thy ſword, thy courage, and thy Art,
For to defend my ſelf, thy better part,
This warineſſe count not for cowardiſe,
He is not truly valiant that's not wiſe.
It's no leſſe glory to defend a town,
Then by aſſault to gain one, not our own
And if *Marcellus* bold, be call d *Romes* ſword,
Wiſe *Fabius* is her buckler. all accord
And if thy haſte, my ſlowneſſe ſhould not temper,
'Twere but a mad, irregular diſtemper;
Enough of that, by our Siſter heretofore,
I'le come to that which wounds me ſomewhat more:
Of Learning, and of Policie, thou would'ſt bereave me,
But's not thy ignorance ſhal thus deceive me.

D   What

What greater Clerke, or polititian lives ?
Then he whose brain a touch my humour gives.
What is too hot, my coldnesse doth abate;
What's diffluent, I do consolidate
If I be partial judg'd, or thought to erre,
The melancholy Snake shal it aver.
Those cold dry heads, more subtilly doth yeild,
Then all the huge beasts of the fertile field.
Thirdly, thou dost confine me to the spleen,
As of that only part I was the Queen:
Let me as wel make thy precincts, the gal,
To prison thee within that ladder smal.
Reduce the man to's principles, then see
If I have not more part, then al ye three
What is without, within, of theirs, or thine.
Yer time and age, shal soon declare it mine.
When death doth seize the man, your stock is left,
When you poor bankrupts prove, then have I most
You'l say, here none shal ere disturbe my right,
You high born (from that lump) then take your flight
Then who s mars friend, when life and all forsakes ?
His mother (mine) him to her wombe retakes,
Thus he is ours, his portion is the grave
But whilst he lives, Ile shew what part I have
And first, the firme dry bones, I justly clum:
The strong foundation of the stately frame
Likewise the useful spleen, though not the best,
Yet is a bowel cal'd wel as the rest
The Lver, Stomach, owes it thanks of right ·
The first it dri nes, o'th' last quicks appetite,
Laughter (though thou sayst malice) flowes from hence,
These two in one cannot have residence.

                                                      Fir

But thou moſt groſly do'ſt miſtake, to thinke
The Spleen for al you three, was made a ſinke,
Of al the reſt, thou'ſt nothing there to do,
But if thou haſt, that malice comes from you.
Again, you often touch my ſwarthy hew,
That black is black, and I am black, tis true,
But yet more comely far, I dare avow,
Then is thy torrid noſe, or braſen brow.
But that which ſhewes how high thy ſpight is bent,
In charging me, to be thy excrement.
Thy loathſome imputation I defie,
So plain a ſlander needeth no reply.
When by thy heat, thou'ſt bak'd thy ſelfe to cruſt,
Thou do'ſt aſſume my name, wel be it juſt,
This transmutation is, but not excretion,
Thou wants Philoſophy, and yet diſcretion.
Now by your leave, Ile let your greatneſſe ſee,
What officer thou art to al us three.
The Kitchin Drudge, the cleanſer of the ſinks,
That caſts out all that nor eates, or drinks.
Thy bittering quality, ſt   retates,
Til filth and thee, nature exhonorates.
If any doubt this truth, whence this ſhould come,
Show them thy paſſage to th' *Duodenum*
If there thou r ſtopt, to th' Liver thou turn'ſt in,
And ſo with jaundiſe, Saffern al the ſkin.
No further time ile ſpend, in confutations,
I truſt I've clear'd your ſlandrous imputations.
I now ſpeake unto al, no more to one,
Pray hear, admire, and learn inſtruction.
My vertues yours ſurpaſſe, without compare .
The firſt, my conſtancy, that jewel rare.

D 2

Choler

Choler's too rash, this golden gift to hold.
And Sanguine is more fickle many fold.
Here, there, her restlesse thoughts do ever flye,
Constant in nothing, but inconstancy,
And what Flegme is, we know, likewise her mother,
Unstable is the one, so is the other.
With me is noble patience also found,
Impatient Choler loveth not the sound.
VVhat Sanguine is, she doth not heed, nor care.
Now up, now down, transported like the Aire
Flegm's patient, because her nature stame.
But I by vertue, do acquire the same.
My temperance, chastity, is eminent,
But these with you are seldome resident.
Now could I stain my ruddy sisters face,
With purple dye, to shew but her disgrace.
But I rather with silence, vaile her shame;
Then cause her blush, while I dilate the same.
Nor are ye free, from this inormity,
Although she beare the greatest obloquie.
My prudence, judgement, now I might reveale,
But wisdome 'tis, my wisdom to conceale.
Unto diseases not inclin'd as ye
Nor cold, nor hot, Ague, nor Plurisie,
Nor Cough, nor Quinsie, nor the burning Feavor.
I rarely feel to act his fierce indevour.
My sicknesse cheifly in conceit doth lye,
What I imagine, that's my malady.
Strange Chymera's are in my phantasie,
And things that never were, nor shal I see
Talke I love not, reason lyes not in length.
Nor multitude of words, argues our strength,

Fo

I've done, pray Sister Flegme procced in course,
We shal expect much sound, but little force.

Flegme.

PAtient I am, patient :'d need to be,
To bear the injurious taunts of three;
Though wit I want, and anger I have lesse,
Enough of both, my wrongs for to expresse;
I've not forgot how bitter Choler spake,
Nor how her Gaul on me the causlesse brake,
Nor wonder 'twas, for hatred there's not smal,
Where opposition is diametrical ·
To what is truth, I freely wil assent,
(Although my name do suffer detriment)
What's slanderous, repel, doubtful, dispute;
And when i've nothing left to say, be mute;
Valour I want, no Souldier am, 'tis true,
I'le leave that manly property to you,
I love no thundering Drums, nor bloody Wars,
My polish'd skin was not ordain'd for skars,
And though the pitched field i've ever fled,
At home, the Conquerours, have conquered:
Nay, *I* could tel you (what's more true then meet)
That Kings have laid their Scepters at my feet,
When sister Sanguine paints my Ivory face,
The Monarchs bend, and sue, but for my grace;
My Lilly white, when joyned with her red,
Princes hath slav'd, and Captains captived
Country with Country, *Greece* with *Asia* fights,
S.x.y nine Princes, all stout *Hero* Knights.

D 3   Under

Under *Troy* wals, ten years wil waſt away,
Rather then looſe, one beauteous *Helleua*;
But 'twere as vain, to prove the truth of mine,
As at noon day to tel, the Sun doth ſhine
Next difference betwixt us twain doth lye,
Who doth poſſeſſe the Brain, or thou, or I;
Shame forc'd thee ſay, the matter that was mine,
But the ſpirits, by which it acts are thine,
Thou ſpeakeſt truth, and I can ſpeak no leſſe,
Thy heat doth much, I candidly confeſſe,
But yet thou art as much, I truly ſay,
Beholding unto me another way.
And though *I* grant, thou art my helper here,
No debtor I, becauſe 'tis paid elſe where,
With all your flouriſhes, now Siſters three,
Who is't or dare, or can compare with me;
My excellencies are ſo great, ſo many,
I am confounded, 'fore I ſpeak of any;
The Brain's the nobleſt member all allow,
The ſcituation, and form wil it avow,
Its ventricles, membranees, and wond'rous net,
Galen, *Hipocrates*, drives to a ſet.
That divine Eſſence, the immortal Soul,
Though it in all, and every part be whole:
Within this ſtately place of eminence,
Doth doub leſſe keep its mighty reſidence,
And ſurely the Soul's ſenſative here lives,
Which life and motion to each Creiture gives,
The conjugations of the parts to th'brain
Doth ſhew, hence ſlowes the power which they retain,
Within th's high built Citadel doth lye,
The Reaſon, Fancy, and the Memory,

                                            The

The faculty of speech doth here abide,
The spirits animal, from whence doth slide,
The five most noble Sences, here do dwel,
Of three, its hard to say, which doth excel;
This point for to discusse longs not to me,
Ile touch the Sight, great'st wonder of the three,
The optick nerve, coats, humours, all are mine,
Both watry, glassie, and the christaline.
O! mixture strange, oh colour, colourlesse,
Thy perfect temperament, who can expresse?
He was no foole, who thought the Soul lay here,
Whence her affections, passions, speak so clear;
O! good, O bad, O true, O traiterous eyes!
What wonderments, within your bals there lyes?
Of all the Sences, Sight shal be the Queen,
Yet some may wish, oh, had mine eyes ne're seene.
Mine likewise is the marrow of the back,
Which runs through all the spondles of the rack,
It is the substitute o'th royal Brain,
All nerves (except seven paire) to it retain;
And the strong ligaments, from hence arise,
With joynt to joynt, the entire body tyes;
Some other parts there issue from the Brain,
Whose use and worth to tel, I must refrain;
Some worthy learned Crooke may these reveal,
But modesty hath charg'd me to conceal,
Here's my epitome of excellence,
For what's the Brains, is mine, by consequence;
A foolish Brain (saith Choler) wanting heat,
But a mad one, say I, where 'tis too great,
Phrensie's worse, then folly, one would more glad,
With a tame foole converse, then with a mad.

D 4   Then

Then , my head for learning is not the fittest,
Ne're did I heare that Choler was the witt'est ,
Thy judgement is unsafe, thy fancy little,
For memory, the sand is not more brittle.
Again, none's fit for Kingly place but thou,
If Tyrants be the best, i'le it allow ;
But if love be, as requisite as feare,
Then I, and thou, must make a mixture here
Wel, to be breif, Choler I hope now's laid,
And I passe by what sister Sanguine said ,
To Melancholly i'le make no reply,
The worst she said, was, instability,
And too much talk, both which, I do confesse,
A warning good, hereafter i'le say lesse
Let's now be freinds, 'tis time our spight was spent,
Lest we too late, this rashnesse do repent,
Such premises wil force a sad conclusion,
Unlesse we 'gree, all fals into confusion.
Let Sanguine, Choler, with her hot hand hold,
To take her moyst, my moistnesse wil be bold ,
My cold, cold Melanchollies hand shal clasp,
Her dry, dry Cholers other hand shal grasp ,
Two hot, two moist, two cold, two dry here be,
A golden Ring, the Posey, *Unity :*
Nor jars, nor scoffs, let none hereafter see,
But all admire our perfect amity ,
Nor be discern'd, here's water, earth, aire, fire,
But here's a compact body, whole, entire :
This loving counsel pleas d them all so wel,
That Flegme was judg'd, for kindnesse to excel.

The Four Ages of Man.

Loe now ' four other acts upon the stage,
Childhood, and Youth, the Manly, and
Old-age.
The first : for unto Flegme,grand-child to
water,
Unstable, supple, moist,and cold, his Naure.
The second, frolick, claimes his pedigree,
From blood and aire, for hot, and moist is he.
The third, of fire, and choler is compos'd,
Vindicative, and quarelsome dispos'd
The last, of earth, and heavy melancholly,
Solid,having all lightnesse, and al folly.
Childhood was cloath'd in white, and given to show,
His spring was intermixed with some snow.
Upon his head a Girland Nature set :
Of Dazy, Primrose, and the Violet.
Such cold mean flowers (as these) blossome betime,
Before the Sun hath throughly warm'd tne clime.
His hobby striding, did not ride, but run,
And in his hand an hour glasse new begun,
In dangers every moment of a fall,
And when tis broke, then ends his life and all.
But if he hold, til it have run its list,
Then may he live, til threescore years or past.

Next

Next, youth came up, in gorgeous attire,
(As that fond age, doth most of al desire.)
His Suit of Crimson, and his Scarfe of Green :
In's countenance, his pride quickly was seen.
Girland of Roses, Pinks, and Gilliflowers,
Seemed to grow on's head (bedew'd with showers)
His face as fresh, as is *Aurora* faire,
When blushing first, she 'gins to red the Aire
No wooden horse, but one of mettal try'd
He seems to flye, or swim, and not to ride
Then prauncing on the Stage, about he wheels;
But as he went, death waited at his heeles.
The next came up, in a more graver sort,
As one that car'd, for a good repo t
His Sword by's side, and choler in his eyes,
But neither us'd (as yet) for he was wise
O Autumne fruits a basket on his arme.
His golden god in's purse, which was his charm:
And last of al, to act upon th s Stag.,
Leaning upon his staffe, comes up old age
Under his arme a Sheife of wheat he bore,
A Harvest of the best, what needs he more.
In's other hand a glasse, ev'n almost run,
This writ about : *This out, then I am done*
His hoary haires, and grave aspect made way;
And al gave eare, to what he had to say.
These being met, each in his equipage,
Intend to speak, according to their age
But wise Old-age, did with all gravity,
To childish childhood, give precedency.
And to the rest, his reason mildly told,
That he was young, before he grew so old

To

To do as he, the reſt ſul ſoon aſſents,
Their method was, that of the Elemen s,
That each ſhou'd tel, what of himſelfe he knew,
Both good and bad, but yet no more then's true
Wrth heed now ſtood, three ages of fraile man,
To hear the child, who crying, thus begen

Childhood.

AH me ! conceiv'd in ſin, and born in ſorrov,
  A nothing, here to day, but gone to morrow.
Whoſe mean beginning, bluſhing cann't reveale,
But night and dark-nelle, moſt with ſhame conceal.
My mothers breeding ſicknes, I will ſpare;
Her nine months weary burden not declare
To ſhew her bearing pangs, I ſhou'd do wrong,
To tel that paine, which cann't be told by tongue;
With tears into this world I did arrive,
My mother ſtil did waſte, as I did thrive:
Who yet with love, and all alacrity,
Spending was willing, to be ſpent for me,
With wayward cryes, I did diſturbe her reſt,
Who ſought ſtil to appeaſe me, with her breſt,
With weary armes, ſhe danc'd, and By, By, ſung,
When wretched I (ungrate) had done the wrong.
When Infancy was paſt, my Childiſhneſſe,
Did act al folly, that it could expreſſe.
My ſillineſſe did only take delight,
In that which riper age did ſcorn, and ſlight.
In Rattles, Bables, and ſuch toyiſh ſtuffe.
My then ambitious thoughts, were low enough.

My high-borne fou'e, fo ftraitly was confin'd ·
That its own worth, it did not know, nor mind.
This little houfe of flefh, did fpacious count;
Through ignorance, all troubles d·d furmount.
Yet this advantage, had mine ignorance,
Freedome from Envy, and from Arrogance.
How to be rich, or great, I did not carke,
A Baron or a Duke, ne'r made my mark.
Nor ftudious was, Kings favours how to buy,
With coftly prefents, or bafe flattery.
No office coveted, wherein I might
Make ftrong my felfe, and turne afide weak righe.
No malice bare, to this, or that great Peer,
Nor unto buzzing whifperots, gave ear.
I gave no hand, nor vote, for death, or life ·
I'd nought to do, 'twixt Prince, and peoples ftrife.
No Statift I. nor Marti'lift i'th' field,
Where e're I went, mine innocence was fhield.
My quarrells, not for Diadems did rife;
But for an Apple, Plumbe, or fome fuch prize,
My ftroks did caufe no death, nor wounds, nor skars.
My little wrath did ceafe foon as my wars.
My duel was no challenge, nor did feek
My foe fhould weltering, with his bowels reck.
I had no Suits at law, neighbours to vex.
Nor evidence for land, did me perplex.
I fear'd no ftormes, nor al the windes that blows,
I had no fhips at Sea, no fraughts to loofe.
I fear'd no drought, nor wer, I had no crop,
Nor yet on future things did place my hope.
This was mine innocence, but oh the feeds,
Lay raked up; of all the curfed weeds,

Which

Which sprouted forth, in my insuing age,
As he can tell, that next comes on the stage.
But yet let me relate, before I go,
The sins, and dangers I am subject to
From birth stayned, with *Adams* sinfull fact;
From thence I 'gan to sin, as soon as act.
A perverse will, a love to what's forbid.
A serpents sting in pleasing face lay hid.
A lying tongue as soon as it could speak,
And fift Commandement do daily break.
Oft stubborn, peevish, sullen, pout, and cry:
Then nought can please, and yet I know not why.
As many was my sins, so dangers too:
For sin brings sorrow, sicknesse, death, and woe.
And though I misse, the tossings of the mind.
Yet griefs, in my fraile flesh, I still do find.
What gripes of wind, mine infancy did pain?
What tortures I, in breeding teeth sustain?
What crudities my cold stomach hath bred?
Whence vomits, wormes, and flux have issued?
What breaches, knocks, and falls I daily have?
And some perhaps, I carry to my grave.
Some times in fire, sometimes in waters fall:
Strangely preserv'd, yet mind it not at all.
At home, abroad, my danger's manifold.
That wonder tis, my glasse till now doth hold.
I've done, unto my elders I give way.
For 'tis but little, that a childe can say.

Youth.

Youth.

MY goodly cloathing, and my beauteous skin,
Declare some greater riches are within ;
But what is best i'le first present to view,
And then the worst, in a more ugly hue ,
For thus to do, we on this Stage assemble,
Then let not him, which hath most craft dissemble ;
Mine education, and my learning's such,
As might my self, and others, profit much :
With nurture trained up in vertues Schools,
Of Science, Arts, and Tongues, I know the rules,
The manners of the Court, I likewise know,
Nor ignorant what they in Country do ;
The brave attempts of valiant Knights I prize,
That dare climbe Battlements, rear'd to the skies ;
The snorting Horse, the Trumpet, Drum I like,
The glistring Sword, and wel advanced Pike ,
I cannot lye in trench, before a Town,
Nor wait til good advice our hopes do crown ;
I scorn the heavy Corslet, Musket proof,
I fly to catch the Bullet that's aloof ;
Though thus in field, at home, to all most k nd,
So affable that I do suit each mind ,
I can insinuate into the brest,
And by my mirth can raise the heart deprest ,
Sweet Musick rapteth my harmonious Soul,
And elevates my thoughts above the Pole
My wit, my bounty, and my courtesie,
Makes all to place their future hopes on me.

This

This is my beft, but youth (is known) alas,
To be as wilde as is the fnuffing Affe,
As vain as froth, as vanity can be,
That who would fee vain man, may look on me :
My gifts abus'd, my education loft,
My woful Parents longing hopes all croft,
My wit, evaporates in meriment
My valour, in fome beaftly quarrel's fpent,
Martial deeds I love not, 'caufe they're vertuous;
But doing fo, migh feem magnanimous.
My Luft doth hurry me, to all that's ill,
I know no Law, nor reafon, but my wil ,
Sometimes lay wait to take a wealthy purfe,
Or ftab the man, in s own defence, that's worfe.
Sometimes I cheat (unkind) a female Heir,
Of all at once, who not fo wife, as fair,
Trufteth my loving looks, and glozing tongue,
Until her freinds, treafure, and honour's gone.
Sometimes I fit caroufing others health,
Until mine own be gone, my wit, and wealth ;
From pipe to pot, from pot to words, and blows,
For he that loveth Wine, wanteth no woes ,
Dayes, nights, with Ruffins, Roarers, Fidlers fpend,
To all obfcenity, my eares I bend.
All counfel hate, which tends to make me wife,
And deareft freinds count for mine enemies ,
If any care I take, 'tis to be fine,
For fure my fuit more then my vertues fhine ,
If any time from company I fpare,
'Tis fpent in curling, trifling up my hair ;
Some young *Adonis* I do ftrive to be,
Sardana Pallus, now furvives in me :

Cards,

Cards, Dice, and Oaths, concomitant, I love,
To Masques, to Playes, to Taverns stil I move,
And in a word, if what I am you'd heare,
Seek out a Brittish, bruitish Cavaleer,
Such wretch, such monster am I, but yet more,
I want a heart all this for to deplore.
Thus, thus alas! I have mispent my time,
My youth, my best, my strength, my bud, and prime:
Remembring not the dreadful day of Doom,
Nor yet that heavy reckoning for to come;
Though dangers do attend me every houre,
And gastly death oft threats me with her power,
Sometimes by wounds in idle combates taken,
Sometimes by Agues all my body shaken,
Sometimes by Feavers, all my moisture drinking,
My heart lyes frying, and my eyes are sinking;
Sometimes the Cough, Stitch, painful Plurisie,
With sad affrights of death, doth menace me,
Sometimes the loathsome Pox, my face be-mars,
With ugly marks of his eternal scars,
Sometimes the Phrensie, strangely madds my Brain,
That oft for it, in *Bedlam* I remain.
Too many's my Diseases to recite,
That wonder 'tis I yet behold the light,
That yet my bed in darknesse is not made,
And I in black oblivions den long laid,
Of Marrow ful my bones, of Milk my breasts,
Ceas'd by the gripes of Serjeant Death's Arrests:
Thus I have said, and what i've said you see,
Child hood and youth is vaine, yea vanity.

Middle Age.

CHildehood and youth, forgot, sometimes I've seen,
And now am grown more staid, that have been green,
What they have done, the same was done by me,
As was their praise, or shame, so mine must be.
Now age is more, more good ye do expect;
But more my age, the more is my defect.
But what's of worth, your eyes shal first behold,
And then a world of drosse among my gold.
When my Wilde Oates, were sown, and ripe, & mown,
I then receiv'd a harvest of mine owne.
My reason, then bad judge, how little hope,
Such empty seed should yeeld a better crop.
I then with both hands, graspt the world together,
Thus out of one extreame, into another.
But yet laid hold, on vertue seemingly,
Who climbes without hold, climbes dangeroufly.
Be my condition mean, I then take paints;
My family to keep, but not for gaines.
If rich, I'm urged then to gather more.
To bear me out i'th' world, and feed the poor,
If a father, then for children must provide;
But if none, then for kindred near ally'd.
If Noble, then mine honour to maintaine.
If not, yet wealth, Nobility can gain,
For time, for place, likewise for each relation,
I wanted not my ready allegation.
Yet all my powers, for self-ends are not spent,
For hundreds blesse me, for my bounty sent.

E

Whose

Whose loynes I've cloth'd, and bellies I have fed,
With mine owne fleece, and with my houshold bread
Yea justice I have done, was I in place;
To chear the good, and wicked to deface.
The proud I crush'd, th' oppressed I set free,
The lyars curb'd but nourisht verity.
Was I a pastor, I my flock did feed:
And gently lead the lambes, as they had need,
A Captain I, with skil I train'd my band,
And shew'd them how, in face of foes to stand.
If a Souldier, with speed I did obey,
As readily as could my Leader say
Was I a laborer, I wrought all day,
As chearfully as ere I took my pay.
Thus hath mine age (in all) sometimes done wel.
Sometimes mine age (in all) been worse then hell.
In meannesse, greatnesse, riches, poverty,
Did toile, did broile; oppress'd, did steal and lye.
Was I as poor, as poverty could be,
Then basenesse was companion unto me.
Such scum, as Hedges, and High-wayes do yeeld,
As neither sow, nor reape, nor plant, nor build.
If to Agricolture, I was ordain'd:
Great labours, sorrows, crosses I sustain'd
The early Cock, did summon but in vaine,
My wakefull thoughts, up to my painefull gaine.
For restlesse day and night, I'm rob'd of sleep,
By cankered care, who centinel doth keep
My weary beast, rest from his toile can find,
But if I rest, the more distrest my mind.
If happinesse my sordidnesse hath found,
'Twas in the crop of my manured ground .

My

My fatted Oxe, and my exuberous Cow,
My fleeced Ewe, and ever farrowing Sow.
To greater things, I never did aspire,
My dunghil thoughts, or hopes, could reach no higher.
If to be rich, or great, it was my fate,
How was I broyl'd with envy, and with hate?
Greater, then was the great'st, was my defire,
And greater ftil, did fet my heart on fire.
If honour was the point, to which I fteer'd;
To run my hull upon difgrace I fear'd,
But by ambitious failes, I was fo carryed,
That over flats, and finds, and rocks I norried,
Oppreft, and funke, and fact, all in my way,
That did oppofe me, to my longed bay.
My thirst was higher, then Nobility.
And oft long'd fore, to tafte on Royalty.
Whence poyfon, Piftols, and dread inftruments,
Have been curft furtherers of mine intents
Nor Brothers, Nephewes, Sons, nor Sires I've fpar'd.
When to a Monarchy, my way they barr'd.
There fet, I rid my felfe ftraight cut of hand.
Of fuch as might my fon, or his withftand.
Then heapt up gold, and riches as the clay;
Which others fcatter, like the dew in *May.*
Sometimes vaine-glory is the only bait,
Whereby my empty fcule, is lur'd and caught.
Be I of worth, of learning, or of parts,
I judge, I fhou'd have room, in all mens hearts.
And envy gnawes, if any do furmount.
I hate for to be had, in fmall account
If *Bias* like, I'm fhipt unto my skin,
I glory in my wealth, I have within.

Thus

Thus good, and bad, and what I am, you see,
Now in a word, what my difeafes be.
The vexing Stone, in bladder and in reines,
Torments me with intollerable paines,
The windy Cholick oft my bowels rend,
To break the darkfome prifon, where it's pend,
The knotty Gout doth fadly torture me,
And the reftraining lame Sciatica,
The Quinfie, and the Feavours, oft diftafte me,
And the Confumption, to the bones doth waft me,
Subject to all Difeafes, that's the truth,
Though fome more incident to age, or youth.
And to conclude, I may not tedious be,
Man at his beft eftate is vanity.

Old Age.

WHat you have been, ev'n fuch have I before,
And all you fay, fay I, and fomething more;
Babes innocence, Youths wildnes I have feen,
And in perplexed Middle-age have bin,
Sicknefle, dangers, and anxieties have paft,
And on this Stage am come to act my laft.
I have bin young, and ftrong, and wife as you,
But now, *Bis pueri fenes*, is too true,
In every Age i've found much vanitie,
An end of all perfection now I fee
It's not my valour, honour, nor my gold,
My ruin'd houfe, now falling can uphold;
It's not my Learning, Rhetorick, wit fo large,
Now hath the power, Deaths Warfare, to difcharge;

It s

It's not my goodly house, nor bed of down,
That can refresh, or ease, if Conscience frown,
Nor from alliance now can I have hope,
But what I have done wel, that is my prop,
He that in youth is godly, wise, and sage,
Provides a staffe for to support his age.
Great mutations, some joyful, and some sad,
In this short Pilgrimage I oft have had;
Sometimes the Heavens with plenty smil'd on me,
Sometimes again, rain'd all adversity;
Sometimes in honour, sometimes in disgrace,
Sometime an abject, then again in place,
Such private changes oft mine eyes have seen,
In various times of state i've also been
I've seen a Kingdom flourish like a tree,
When it was rul'd by that Celestial she;
And like a Cedar, others so surmount,
That but for shrubs they did themselves account,
Then saw I *France*, and *Holland* sav'd, *Cales* won,
And *Philip*, and *Albertus*, half undone;
I saw all peace at home, terror to foes,
But ah, I saw at last those eyes to close.
And then, me thought, the world at noon grew dark,
When it had lost that radiant Sun-like spark,
In midst of greifs, I saw some hopes revive,
(For 'tis our hopes then kept our hearts alive)
I saw hopes dasht, our forwardnesse was shent,
And silenc'd we, by Act of Parliament.
I've seen from *Rome*, an execrable thing,
A plot to blow up Nobles, and their King,
I've seen designes at *Ree*, and *Cades* crost,
And poor I [alatinate] for ever lost;

E 3

I've

I've seen a Prince, to live on others lands,
A Royall one, by almes from Subjects hands,
I've seen base men, advanc'd to great degree,
And worthy ones, put to extremity.
But not their Princes love, nor state so high;
could once reverse, their shamefull destiny.
I've seen one stab'd, another loose his head,
And others fly their Country, through their dread
I've seen, and so have ye, for 'tis but late,
The desolation, of a goodly State.
Plotted and acted, so that none can tell,
Who gave the counsel, but the Prince of hell.
I've seen a land unmoulded with great paine.
But yet may live, to see't made up again.
I've seen it shaken, rent, and soak'd in blood,
But out of troubles, ye may see much good,
These are no old wives tales, but this is truth,
We o'd men love to tell, what's done in youth.
But I returne, from whence I stept awry,
My memory is short, and braine is dry.
My Almond-tree (gray haires) doth flourish now,
And back, once straight, begins apace to bow
My grinders now are few, my sight doth faile
My skin is wrinkled, and my cheeks are pale
No more rejoyce, at musickes pleasant noyse,
But do awake, at the cocks changing voyce
I cannot scent, savours of pleasant meat,
Nor sipors find, in what I drink or eat
My hands and armes, once strong, have lost their might,
I cannot labour, nor I cannot fight·
My comely legs as nimble as the Roe,
Now stiffe and numb, can hardly creep or go.

My

My heart sometimes as fierce, as Lion bold,
Now trembling, and fearful, sad, and cold ;
My golden Bowl, and silver Cord, e're long,
Shal both be broke, by wracking death so strong ;
I then shal go, whence I shal come no more,
Sons, Nephews, leave, my death for to deplore ;
In pleasures, and in labours, I have found.
That earth can give no consolation sound.
To great, to rich, to poore, to young, or old,
To mean, to noble, fearful, or to bold·
From King to begger, all degrees shal finde
But vanity, vexation of the minde ,
Yea knowing much, the pleasant'st life of all,
Hath yet amongst that sweet, some bitter gail.
Though reading others Works, doth much refresh,
Yet studying much, brings wearinesse to th' flesh.
My studies, labours, readings, all are done,
And my last period now e'n almost run ,
Corruption, my Father, I do call,
Mother, and sisters both, the worms, that crawl,
In my dark house, such kindred I have store,
There, I shal rest, til heavens shal be no more ,
And when this flesh shal rot, and be consum'd,
This body, by this soul, shal be assum'd ,
And I shal see, with these same very eyes,
My strong Redeemer, comming in the skies ;
Triumph I shal, o're Sin, o're Death, o're Hel,
And in that hope, I bid you all farewel.

The

The four Seasons of the Yeare.

Spring.

ANother Four i've yet for to bring on,
Of four times four, the last quaternion,
The Winter, Summer, Autumne, and the
Spring,
In season all these Seasons I shal bring;
Sweet Spring, like man in his minority,
At present claim'd, and had priority,
With smiling Sun shine face, and garment, green,
She gently thus began, like some fair Queen,
Three months there are allotted to my share,
March, April, May, of all the rest most faire,
The tenth o'th' first *Sol* into *Aries* enters,
And bids defiance to all tedious Winters:
And now makes glad those blinded Northern wights,
Who for some months have seen out starry lights,
Crosses the Line, and equals night and day,
Stil adds to th' last, til after pleasant *May*;
Now goes the Plow-man to his merry toyl,
For to unloose his Winter-locked soyl,
The Seeds-man now doth lavish out his Grain,
In hope, the more he casts, the more to gain;
The Gardner, now superfluous branches lops,
And Poles erects, for his green clambering Hops;
Now digs, then sows, his hearbs, his flowers, and roots,
And carefully manures his trees of fruits.

The

The Pleiades, their influence now give,
And all that seem'd as dead, afresh do live.
The croaking Frogs, whom nipping Winter kild,
Like Birds, now chirp, and hop about the field;
The Nitingale, the Black-bird, and the Thrush,
Now tune their layes, on sprays of every bush;
The wanton frisking Kids, and soft fleec'd Lambs,
Now jump, and play, before their feeding Dams,
The tender tops of budding Grasse they crop,
They joy in what they have, but more in hope,
For though the Frost hath lost his binding power,
Yet many a fleece of Snow, and stormy showre,
Doth darken *Sols* bright face, makes us remember
The pinching Nor-west cold, of fierce *December*.
My second month is *April*, green, and fair,
Of longer dayes, and a more temperate air;
The Sun now keeps his posting residence
Ih *Taurus* Signe, yet hasteth straight from thence;
For though in's running progresse he doth take
Twelve houses of the oblique Zodiack,
Yet never minute still was known to stand,
But only once at *Joshua's* strange command;
This is the month whose fruitfull showers produces
All Plants, and Flowers, for all delights, and uses,
The Pear, the Plumbe, and Apple-tree now flourish,
And Grasse growes long, the tender Lambs to nourish;
The Primrose pale, and azure Violet,
Among the verduous Grasse hath Nature set,
That when the Sun (on's love) the earth doth shine,
These might as Lace, set out her Garments fine,
The fearful Bird, his little house now builds,
In trees, and wals, in citties, and in fields,

The

'The outside strong, the inside warme and neat.
A natural Artificer compleate.
The clocking hen, her chipping brood now leads,
With wings, and beak, defends them from the gleads.
My next, and last, is pleasant fruitfull *May*,
Wherein the earth, is clad in rich aray:
The sun now enters, loving *Gemine*,
And heats us with, the glances of his eye,
Our Winter rayment, makes us lay aside,
Least by his fervor, we be terrifi'd,
All flowers before the sun-beames now discloses,
Except the double Pinks, and matchlesse Roses.
Now swarmes the busie buzzing hony Bee.
Whose praise deserves a page, from more then me.
The cleanly huswives Diry, now's ith' prime,
Her shelves, and Firkins fil'd for winter time.
The Meads with Cowslip, Hony-suckl's dight,
One hangs his head, the other stands upright.
But both rejoyce, at th' heavens clear smiling face,
More at her showers, which water them a space.
For fruits, my season yeelds, the early Cherry,
The hasty Pease, and wholesome red Strawberry,
More solid fruits, require a longer time.
Each season, hath his fruit, so hath each clime.
Each man his owne peculiar excellence,
But none in all that hath preheminence.
Some subject, shallow braines, much matter yeelds,
Sometime a theame that's large, proves barren fields.
Melodious Spring, with thy short pittance flye,
In this harsh strain, I find no melody,
Yet above all, this priviledge is thine,
Thy dayes stil lengthen, without least decline.

Summ'r

Summer.

WHen Spring had done, then Summer must begin,
  With melted tauny face, and garments thinne.
Refembling choler, fire and middle age;
As Spring did aire, blood, youth in's equipage.
Wiping her fweat from off her brow, that ran,
VVith haire all wet, fhe puffing thus began.
Bright *June*, *July*, and *August*, hot are mine,
Ith' firft, *Sol* doth in crabed *Cancer* fhine.
His progreffe to the North, now's fully done,
And retrograde, now is my burningSun
VVho to his Southward tropick ftill is bent,
Yet doth his parching heat the mere augment,
The reafon why, becaufe his flames fo faire,
Hath formerly much heat, the earth and aire.
Like as an oven, that long time hath been heat.
Whofe vehemency, at length doth grow fo great,
That if you do, remove her burning ftore,
She s for a time as fervent as before
Now go thofe frolick fwaines, the fhepheard lad,
To wafh their thick cloath'd flocks, with pipes ful glad.
In the coole ftreames they labour with delight,
Rubbing their dirty coates, till they look white.
Whofe fleece when purely fpun, and deeply dy'd,
With robes thereof, Kings have been dignifi'd.
'Mongft all ye fhepheards, never but one man,
Was like th e noble, brave *Archadian*.
Yet hath your life, made Kings the fame envy,
Though you repofe on graffe under the skye.

Carelesse

Carelesse of worldly wealth, you sit and pipe,
Whilst they're imbroyl'd in Wars, and troubles ripe,
Which made great *Bajazet* cry out in's woes,
O'! happy Shepheard, which had not to lose.
Or *hobulus*, nor yet *Sebastia* great,
But whist'leth to thy Flock in cold, and heat,
Viewing the Sun by day, the Moon by night,
Endimions, Diana's dear delight ;
This Month the Roses are distill'd in Glasses,
whose fragrant scent, all made-perfume surpasses,
The Cherry, Goos-berry, is now i'th prime,
And for all sorts of Pease this is the time.
July my next, the hot'st in all the year,
The Sun in *Leo* now hath his carrear,
Whose flaming breath doth melt us from afar,
Increased by the Star *Canicular*,
This month from *Julius Cæsar* took the name,
By *Romans* celebrated to his fame
Now go the Mowers to their slashing toyl,
The Medows of their burden to dispoyl,
With weary stroaks, they take all in their way,
Bearing the burning heat of ne long day,
The Forks, and Rakes do follow them amain,
Which makes the aged fields look young again,
The groaning Carts to bear away this prise.
To Barns, and Stacks, where it for Folder lyes.
My next, and last, is *August*, fiery hot,
For yet the South-ward Sun abateth not,
This month he keeps with *Virgo* for a space,
The dryed earth is parched by his face.
August, of great *Augustus* took its name,
Romes second Emperour of peaceful fame ;

With

With Sickles now, the painful Reapers go,
The ruffling treffe of *ferra* for to moe,
And bundles up in fheaves the weighty Wheat,
Which after Manchet's made, for Kings to eat,
The Barley, and the Rye, fhould firft had place,
Although their Bread have not fo white a face.
The Carter leads all home, with whiftling voyce,
He plow'd with pain, but reaping doth rejoyce,
His fweat, his toyl, his careful, wakeful nights,
His fruitful crop, abundantly requites.
Now's ripe the Pear, Pear-plumbe, and Apricock,
The Prince of Plumbs, whofe ftone is hard as Rock
Tho Summer's fhort, the beauteous Autumne haftes,
To fhake his fruit, of moft delicious taftes,
Like good Old Age, whofe younger juycie roots,
Hath ftil afcended up in goodly Fruits,
Until his head be gray, and ftreng h be gone,
Yet then appears the worthy deeds he 'ath done:
To feed his boughes, exhaufted hath his fap,
Then drops his Fruits into the Eaters lap.

Autumne.

OF Autumne months, *September* is the prime,
Now day and night are equal in each clime,
The tenth of this, *Sol* rifeth in the Line,
And doth in poyzing *Libra* this month fhine.
The Vintage now is ripe, the Grapes are preft,
Whofe lively liquor oft is curft, and bleft,
For nought's fo good, but it may be abufed,
But its a precious juyce, when wel it's ufed.

The Raisins now in clusters dryed be,
The Orange, Lemon, Dangle on the tree ;
The Figge is ripe, the Pomgranet also,
And Apples now their yellow sides do show ,
Of Medlar, Quince, of Warden, and of Peach,
The season s now at hand, c‘ ‘l, and each ;
Sure at this time, Time first ‘ began,
And in this month was made ╷ ꞗstate man ;
Fo▪ben in *Eden* was not only seen
Boughs full of leaves, or fruits, but raw, and green,
Or withered stocks, all dry, and dead,
But trees with goodly fruits replenished ,
Which shewes, nor Summer, Winter, nor the Spring,
Great *Adam* was of Paradice made King.
October is my next, we heare in this,
The Northern Winter bl ^ ‘ egin to hisse ,
In *Scorpio* resideth now th ╷
And his declining heat is almost ꝺone
The fruitful trees, all withered now do stand,
Who‘e yellow saplesse leaves by winds are fann’d
Wh ch notes, when youth, and strength, have past their
D crepit age must also have its time ,　　　　(prime,
The sap doth slily creep towards the earth,
Th╵re rests, untill the Sun give it a birth .
So doth Old Age stil tend unto his Grave,
Whe e also he, his Winter time must have ,
But when the Son of Righteousnesse drawes nigh,
His dead old stoc , again shall mount on high
November is my last, for time doth haste,
We now of Winters sharp﹐ sse ’gun to taste;
This month’s the Sun in *Sagittarius*,
So farre remote, his glances warm not us ,

Almost

Almost at shortest is the shortned day,
The Northern Pole beholdeth not one ray.
Now *Green land*, *Groen-land*, *Lap-land*, *Fin-land*, see
No Sun, to lighten their obscurity;
Poor wretches, that in total darknesse lye,
With minds more dark, then is the darkned sky;
This month is timber for all uses fell'd,
When cold, the sap to th' roots hath low'st repell'd;
Beef, Brawn, and Pork, are now in great'st request,
And solid'st meats, our stomachs can digest,
This time warm cloaths, sul dier, and good fires,
Our pinched flesh, and empty panch requires:
Old cold, dry age, and earth, Autumne resembles,
And melancholy, which most of all dissembles.
I must be short, and short's, t' shortned day,
What Winter hath to tel, now let him say.

Winter.

COld, moist, young, flegmy Winter now doth lye
In Swadling clouts, like new born infancy,
Bound up with Frosts, and furr'd with Hails, and
Ard like an Infant, stil he taller growes.   (Snows,
December is the first, and now the Sun
To th' Southword tropick his swift race hath run,
This month he's heus'd in horned *Capricorn*,
From thence he 'gins to length the shortned morn,
Through Christendome, with great festivity
Now's held, a Guest, (bot blest) Nativity
Cold frozen *January* next comes in,
Chilling the blood, and shrinking up the skin.

In

In *Aquarius*, now keeps the loved Sun,
And North-ward his unwearied race doth run ;
The day much longer then it was before,
The cold not lessened, but augmented more.
Now toes, and eares, and fingers often freeze,
And Travellers sometimes their noses leese.
Moyst snowie *February* is my last,
I care not how the Winter time doth haste ;
In *Pisces* now the golden Sun doth shine,
And North ward stil approaches to the Line ;
The Rivers now do ope, and Snows do melt,
And some warm glances from the Sun are felt,
Which is increased by the lengthened day,
Until by's heat be driven all cold away.

My Subjects bare, my Brains are bad,
Or better Lines you should have had ;
The first fell in so naturally,
I could not tell how to passe't by :
The last, though bad, I could not mend,
Accept therefore of what is penn'd,
And all the faults which you shall spy,
Shall at your feet for pardon cry.

Your dutifull Daughter.

A. B.

The

The Foure Monarchies,

the *Aſſyrian* being the firſt, beginning under *Nimrod*, 131. yeares after the Floud.

When Time was young, and World in infancy,
Man did not ſtrive for Soverignty,
But each one thought his petty rule was high,
If of his houſe he held the Monarchy.
This was the Golden Age, but after came
The boyſterous Sons of *Cuſh*, Grand-child to *Ham*,
That mighty Hunter, who in his ſtrong toyls,
Both Beaſts and Men ſubjected to his ſpoyls.
The ſtrong foundation of proud *Babel* laid,
Erech, *Acad*, and *Calneh* alſo made,
Theſe were his firſt, all ſtood in *Shinar* land,
From thence he went *Aſſiria* to command,
And mighty *Ninive*, he there begun,
Not finiſhed, til he his race had run ;
Reſen, *Caleh*, and *Rehoboth* likewiſe,
By him, to Cities eminent did riſe,
Of *Saturn*, he was the original,
Whom the ſucceeding times a god did call,

F

When thus with rule he had been dignified,
One hundred fourteen years, he after dyed.

Bellus.

GReat *Nimrod* dead, *Bellus* the next, his Son,
Confirmes the rule his Father had begun,
  Whose acts, and power, is not for certainty,
Left to the world, by any History,
But yet this blot for ever on him lyes,
He taught the people first to Idolize,
Titles divine, he to himself did take,
Alive, and dead, a god they did him make;
This is that *Bell*, the *Challees* worshipped,
Whose Preists, in Stories, oft are mentioned;
This is that *Bell*, to whom the *Israelites*
So oft profanely offered sacred rites,
This is *Belzebub*, god of *Ekronites*,
Likewise *Bal-peor*, of the *Moabites:*
His reign was short, for as I calculate,
At twenty five, ended his regal date.

Ninus.

HIs father dead, *Ninus* begins his reign,
Transfers his Seat, to the *Assyrian* plain,
  And mighty *Ninivie* more mighty made,
Whose foundation was, by his Grand-sire laid,
Four hundred forty Furlongs, wall'd about,
On which stood fifteen hundred towers stout.

                                          The

The walls one hundred sixty foot upright,,
So broad, three Chariots run abrest there might,
Upon the pleasant banks of *Tigrs* flood,
This stately seat of warlike *Ninus* stood.
This *Ninus* for a god, his father canoniz'd,
To whom the sottish people sacrific'd ;
This Tyrant did his neighbours all oppresse,
Where e're he warr'd he had too good successe,
Barzanes, the great *Armenian* King,
By force, his tributary, he did bring.
The *Median* country, he did also gain,
Pharnus, their King, he caused to be slain ;
An army of three Millions he led out,
Against the *Bactrians* (but that I doubt)
Zoroaster, their King, he likewise slew,
And all the greater *Asia* did subdue,
Semiramis from *Menon* he did take,
Then drown himself, did *Menon*, for her sake ;
Fifty two years he reign'd (as we are told)
The world then was two thousand nineteen old.

Semiramis.

THis great oppressing *Ninus* dead, and gone,
His wife, *Semiramis*, usurp'd the throne,
   She like a brave Virago, play'd the rex,
And was both shame, and glory of her sex,
Her birth-place was *Philistius Ascalon*,
Her Mother *Dogeta*, a Curtezan ,
Others report, she was a vestal Nun,
Adjudg'd to be crown'd, for what she'd done ;

       Trans-

Transform'd into a fish, by Venus will,
Her beauteous face (they feign) retaining still
Sure from this fiction, Dagon first began,
Changing his womans face, into a man.
But all agree, that from no lawfull bed;
This great renowned Empresse, issued.
For which, she was obscurely nourished.
Whence rose that fable, she by birds was fed.
This gallant dame, unto the *Bactrian* war,
Accompaning her husband *Menon* far,
Taking a towne, such valour she did show,
That *Ninus* of her, amorous on did grow;
And thought her fit, to make a Monarch's wife,
Which was the cause poor *Menon* lost his life,
She flourishing with *Ninus*, long did reigne,
Till her ambition, caus'd him to be slaine.
That having no compeer, she might rule all,
Or else she sought, revenge for *Menons* fall:
Some think the *Greeks*, this slander on her cast,
As of her life, licencious, and unchast
And that her worth, deserved no such blame,
As their aspersions, cast upon the same.
But were her vertues, more, or lesse, or none,
She for her potency, must go alone
Her wealth she shew'd, in building *Babylon*,
Admir'd of all, but equaliz'd of none.
These walls so strong, and curiously were wrought;
The after ages, skil, by them were taught.
With Towers, and Bulwarks made of costly stone
Quadrangle was the forme, it stood upon
Each Square, was fifteen thousand paces long,
A hundred gates, it had, of mettall strong.

Three

Three hundred sixty foot, the walls in heighth:
Almost incredible, they were in breadth
Most writers say, six chariots might a front,
With great facility, march safe upon't.
About the wall, a ditch so deep and wide,
That like a river, long it did abide.
Three hundred thousand men, here day, by day,
Bestow'd their labour, and receiv'd their pay,
But that which did, all cost, and art excell,
The wondrous Temple was, she rear'd to *Bell*,
Which in the midst, of this brave Town was plac'd,
(Continuing, till *Xerxes* it defac'd)
Whose stately top, beyond the clouds did rise,
From whence, Astrologers, oft view'd the skies.
This to discribe, in each particular,
A structure rare, I should but rudely marre,
Her gardens, bridges, arches, mounts, and spires;
All eyes that saw, or ears that hears, admires.
On *Shinar* plain, by the *Euphratian* flood,
This wonder of the world, this *Babell* stood
An expedition to the East she made.
Great King *Staurobates*, for to invade.
Her Army of four Millions did consist,
(Each man beleive it, as his fancy list)
Her Camells, Chariots, Gallyes in such number,
As puzzells best hystorians to remember :
But this is marvelous, of all those men,
(They say) but twenty, ere came back agen.
The River *Indus* swept them half away,
The rest *Staurobates* in fight did slay
This was last progresse of this mighty Queen,
Who in her Coun ry never mo e was seen

F 3   The

The Poets feign her turn'd into a Dove,
Leaving the world, to *Venus*, soar'd above,
Which made the *Affyrians* many a day,
A Dove within their Enfigne to difplay.
Forty two years fhe reign'd, and then fhe dy'd,
But by what means, we are not certifi'd.

Ninias, or Zames.

HIs Mother dead, *Ninias* obtains his right,
A Prince wedded to eafe, and to delight,
Or elfe was his obedience very great,
To fit, thus long (obfcure) wrong'd of his feat ;
Some write, his Mother puts his habite on,
Which made the people think they ferv'd her Son ,
But much it is, in more then forty years,
This fraud, in war, nor peace, it all appears ,
It is more like, being with pleafures fed,
He fought no rule, til fhe was gone, and dead ;
What then he did, of worth, can no man tel,
But is fuppos'd to be that *Amraphel*,
Who warr'd with *Sodoms*, and *Gomorahs* King,
'Gainft whom his trained Bands *Abram* did bring.
Some may object, his Parents ruling all,
How he thus fuddenly fhould be thus fmall ?
This anfwer may fuffice, whom it wil pleafe,
He thus voluptuous, and given to eafe,
Each wronged Prince, or childe that did remain,
Would now advantage take, their own to gain ,
So Province, after Province, rent awry,
Until that potent Empire did decay.

Again, the Country was left bare (there is no doubt)
Of men, and wealth, his mother carried out ,
Which to Ler neighbours, when it was made known,
Did then incite, them to regain their own.
What e're he was, they did, or how it fel,
We may suggest our thoughts, but cannot tel ,
For *Ninus*, and all his Race are left,
In deep oblivion, of acts bereft,
And eleav'n hundred of years in silence fit,
Save a few names anew, *Berosus* writ.
And such as care not, what befals their fames,
May feign as many acts, as he did names ;
It is enough, if all be true that s past,
T' *Sardanapalus* next we wil make haste.

Sardanapalus.

SArdanapalus, (Son t' *Ocrazapes*)
Who wallow ed in all voluptuousnesse,
   That palliardizing fot, that out of doores
Ne re shew'd his face, but revell'd with his Whores,
Did wear their garb, their gestures imitate,
And their kind t' excel did emulate.
Knowing his basenesse, and the peoples hate,
Kept ever close, fearing some dismal fate ;
At last *Arbaces* brave, unwarily,
His master like a Strumpet chanc'd to spy,
His manly heart disdained, in the least.
Longer to serve this Metamorphos'd beast,
Unto *Belesus*, then he brake his minde,
Who sick of his disease, he soone did finde.

F 4

Thefe

These two rul'd *Media* and *Babylon*,
Both, for their King, held their dominion,
Belosus, promised *Arbaces* aide,
Arbaces him, fully to be repaid
The last, the *Medes* and *Persians* doth invite.
Against their monstrous King to bring their might,
Belosus the *Chaldeans* doth require,
And the *Arabians*, to further his desire.
These all agree, and forty thousand make,
The rule from their unworthy Prince to take.
By prophesie, *Belosus* strength's their hands,
Arbaces must be master of their lands.
These Forces mustered, and in array,
Sardanapalus leaves his Apish play,
And though of wars, he did abhor the sight,
Fear of his diadem, did force him fight :
And either by his valour, or his fate,
Arbaces courage he did sore abate.
That in dispaire, he left the field and fled
But with fresh hopes *Belosus* succoured.
From *Bactaru* an Army was at hand,
Prest for this service, by the Kings command,
These with celerity, *Arbaces* meets,
And with all termes of amity, he greets,
Makes promises, their necks for to un-yoak,
And their Taxations sore, all to revoake,
T'infranchise them, to grant what they could crave,
To want no priviledge, Subjects should have,
Only intreats them, joyn their force with his,
And win the Crown, which was the way to blisse,
Won by his loving looks, more loving speech,
T'accept of what they could, they him beseech.

Both

Both sides their hearts, their hands their bands unite,
And set upon their Princes Camp that night,
Who revelling in Cups, sung care away,
For victory obtain'd the other day,
But all surpris'd, by this unlookt for fright,
Bereft of wits, were slaughtered down right
The King his Brother leaves, all to sustain,
And speeds himself to *Ninivie* amain,
But *Salmeus* slaine, his Army fals,
The King's pursu'd unto the City wals,
But he once in, pursuers came too late,
The wals, and gates, their course did terminate;
There with all store he was so wel provided,
That what *Arbaces* did, was but derided,
Who there incamp'd two years, for little end,
But in the third, the River prov'd his friend,
Which through much rain, then swelling up so high,
Part of the wal it level caus'd to lye;
Arbaces marches in, the town did take,
For few, or none, did there resistance make;
And now they saw fulfill'd a Prophesie,
That when the River prov'd their enemy,
Their strong wall'd town should suddenly be taken,
By this accomplishment, their hearts were shaken.
Sardanapalus did not seek to fly,
This his inevitable destiny,
But all his wealth, and friends, together gets,
Then on himself, and them, a fire he lets,
This the last Monarch was, of *Ninus* race,
Which for twelve hundred years had held that place;
Twenty one reign'd, same time, as Stories tel,
That *Amaziah* was King of *Ifrae*,

H₃

His Father was then King (as we ſuppoſe)
When *Jonah* for their ſins denounc'd ſuch woes ;
He did repent, therefore it was not done,
But was accompliſhed now, in his Son
Arbaces thus, of all becomming Lord,
Ingeniouſly with each did keep his word ;
Of *Babylon*, *Beloſus* he made King,
With over-plus of all treaſures therein,
To *Bactrians*, he gave their liberty,
Of *Ninivites*, he cauſed none to dye,
But ſuffered, with goods to go elſewhere,
Yet would not let them to inhibite there ,
For he demoliſhed that City great,
And then to *Medii* transfer'd his ſeat
Thus was the promiſe bound, ſince firſt he crav'd,
Of *Meds*, and *Perſians*, their aſſiſting aide ,
A while he, and his race, aſide muſt ſtand,
Not pertinent to what we have in hand,
But *Belochus* in's progeny purſue,
Who did this Monarchy begin anew

Beloſus, or *Belochus*.

BEloſus ſetled, in his new, old ſeat,
Not ſo content, but aiming to be great,
Incroached ſtil upon the bord'ring Lands,
Til *Meſopotamia* he got in's hands,
And either by compound, or elſe by ſtrength,
Aſſyria he alſo gain'd at length ,
Then did rebuild deſtroyed *Ninive*,
A coſtly work, which none could doe but he,

Who

Who own'd the treasures of proud *Babylon*,
And those which seem'd with *Sardanapal's* gone,
But though his Palace, did in ashes lye,
The fire, those Metals could not damnifie;
From rubbish these, with diligence he rakes,
Arbaces suffers all, and all he takes
He thus inricht, by this new tryed gold,
Raises a Phœnix new, from grave o'th old;
And from this heap did after Ages see,
As fair a Town, as the first *Ninivee*.
When this was built, and all matters in peace,
Molests poor *Israel*, his wealth t'encrease.
A thousand talents of *Menahem* had,
Who to be rid of such a guest, was glad,
In sacred Writ, he's known by name of *Pul*,
Which makes the world of differences so full,
That he, and *Belochus*, one could not be,
But circumstance, doth prove the verity;
And times of both computed, so fall out,
That those two made but one, we need not doubt:
What else he did, his Empire to advance,
To rest content we must, in ignorance.
Forty eight years he reign'd, his race then ran,
He left his new got Kingdoms to his Son.

Tiglath Palasser.

BElosus dead, *Tiglath* his warlike Son
Now treads the steps, by which his Father won.
Damsco, ancient seat of famous Kings,
Under subjection by his sword he brings,

Refin their valiant King, he also flew,
An *Syria* t' obedience did subdue ;
Iud 's bad King occasioned this War
When *Resin* force his borders fore did mar.
And divers Cities, by strong hand did feize,
To *Tiglath* then doth *Ahz* fend for eafe.
The temple robes, fo to fulfill his ends,
And to *Affyria*'s King a Prefent fends.
I am thy Servant, and thy Son (quoth he)
From *Rzin*, and from *Pekah* fet me free :
Gladly doth *Tiglah* this advantage take,
And fuccours *Ahz*, yet for *Tiglath's* fake,
When *Rezin*'s flain, his Army over thrown,
Syria he makes a Province of his own.
Unto *Damafcus* then, comes *Iudah*'s King,
His humble thankfulnefs (with haft) to bring,
Acknowledging th' *Affyrians* high defert,
To whom he ought all loyalty of heart
But *Tiglath* having gain'd his wifhed end,
Proves unto *Ahz* but a feigned friend ,
All *Ifraels* Land beyond *Iordan*, he takes
In *Gailec*, he woful havock makes ;
Through *Syria* now he marcht, none ftopt his way,
And *Ahz* open, at his mercy lay,
Who ftil implor'd his love, but was diftreff'd,
(This was that *Ahz*, which fo much tranfgreft)
Thus *Tiglath* reign'd, and wan'd, twen y feven years,
Then by his death, releas'd, was *Ifraels* fears.

Salma-

Salmanasser, or *Nalonasser.*

Tiglath deceas'd, *Salmanasser* is next,
He *Israelites,* more then his Father vext;
*Hosea,*their last King,he did invade,
And him six years his tributary made;
But weary of his servitude, he sought,
To *Ægypts* King, which did avail him nought;
For *Salmanasser,* with a mighty Hoast,
Besieg'd his regal town,and spoyl'd his Coast,
And did the people, nobles, and their King,
Into perpetual thraldome that time bring;
Those that from *Joshua's* time had been Estate, [10 *years.*
Did Justice now, by him, eradicate:
This was that strange degenerated brood,
On whom, nor threats, nor mercies could do good;
Laden with honour prisoners,and with spoyl,
Returns triumphant Victor to his soyl;
Plac'd *Israel n's* Land, where he thought best,
Then sent his Colonies, theirs to invest,
Thus *Iacobs* Sons,in exile must remain,
And pleasant *Canaan* ne're see again ·
Where now those ten Tribes are,can no man tel,
Or how they fare, rich, poor, or ill, or wel;
Whether the *Indians* of the East, or West,
Or wild *Tartarians,* as yet ne're blest,
Or else those *Chinoes* rare, whose wealth, and Arts,
Hath bred more wonder, then beleefe in hearts,
But what, or where they are, yet know not h s,
They shall return, and *Zior* see, with blisse.
Sennacher.

Senacherib.

Senacherib *Salmaneser* succeeds,
Whose haughty heart is shewn in works, and deeds ;
this Was none better then himself can boast,
On *Henah, Arpad,* and on *Ivah* least ;
On H*ena*'s, and on *Sepharuaim's* gods,
'Twixt them and *Israels* he knew no odds.   [7 years.
Until the thundring hand of heaven he felt,
Which made his Army into nothing melt ;
With shame then turn'd to *Ninivie* again,
And by his Sons in's Idols house was slain.

Essarhadon.

His Son, weak *Essarhadon* reign'd in's place,
The fifth, and last, of great *Belosus* race ,
Brave *Merodach,* the Son of *Balladan,*
In *Babylon,* Leiutenant to this man,
Of opportunity advantage takes,
And on his Masters ruins, his house makes ;
And *Belosus*, first, his did unthrone,
So he's now stil'd, the King of *Babylon* ;
After twelve years did *Essarhadon* dye,
And *Merodach* assume the Monarchy.

Merodach

Merodach Baladan.

ALl yeelds to him, but *Ninivie* kept free,
Until his Grand-childe made her bow the knee;
Embaſſadours to *Hezekiah* ſent,   [21 years.
His health congratulates with complement.

Ben. Merodach.

BEn. *Merodach*, Succeſſor to this King,
Of whom is little ſaid in any thing;   [22 years.
But by conjecture this, and none but he,
Led King *Manaſſeh*, to captivity.

Nebulaſſar.

BRave *Nebulaſſar* to this King was Sonne,
The ancient *Niniveh* by him was won,
For fifty years, or more, it had been free,
Now yeelds her neck unto captivity :   [12 years.
A Vice-roy from her foe, ſhe's glad t'accept,
By whom in firm obedience ſhe's kept.

Nebuchadnezar, or *Nebopolaſſar:*

THe famous Wars, of this Heroyick King,
Did neither *Homer*, *Heſiole*, *Virgil* ſing,

Nor

Nor of his acts have we the certainty,
From some t*incul des* grave History;
No 's Metamorphosis from *Ovids* Book,
Nor his restoring from old legends took;
But by the Prophets, Pen-men most Divine,
This Prince in's magnitude doth ever shine;
This was of Monarchies that head of gold,
The richest, and the dreadful'st to behold,
Th s was that tree, whose branches fill'd the earth,
Under whose shadow, birds, and beasts, had birth,
This was that King of Kings, did what he pleas'd,
Kild, sav d, pull'd down, set up, or pain'd, or eas'd,
And this is he   who when he fear'd the least,
Was turned from a King, unto a Beast,
This Prince, the last year of his Fathers reign,
Against *Ichoiakim* marcht with his train,
Iudah s p-or King besieg'd, wh succourlesse,
Yeelds to h s mercy, and the present stresse;
His Vassal is, gives pledges for h s truth,
Children of Royal bloud, unblemish'd youth,
Wise *Daniel*, and his fellows 'mongst the rest,
By the victorious King to *Babel's* prest,
The temple of rich ornaments defac'd,
And in his Idols house the Vass ls plac'd.
The next year he, with unresisted hand,
Quite vanquish'd *Pharaoh* Necho, and his Band,
By great E*uphrates* did h s Army fail,
Which was the losse of *Syria* withall,
Then into Ægypt, Necho did retire,
Which in few years proves the *Assyrars* hire,
A mighty Army next, he doth prepare,
And unto wealthy *Tire* with hast repaire.

Such was the scituation of this place,
As might not him, but all the world out face;
That in her pride, she knew not which to boast,
Whether her wealth, or yet her strength was most ;
How in all Merchandise she did excell,
None but the true *Ezekiel* need to tell ·
And for her strength, how hard she was to gain,
Can *Babels* tired Souldiers tell wit'h pain ;
Within an Island had this City seat,
Divided from the maine, by channel great ›
Of costly Ships, and Gallies, she had store,
And Mariners, to handle sayle, and oare ;
But the *Chaldeans* had nor ships, nor skill;
Their shoulders must their Masters minde fulfil ;
Fetch rubbish from the opposite old rown,
And in the channell throw each burden down ;
Where after many assayes, they make at last,
The Sea firm Land, whereon the Army past,
And took the wealthy town, but all the gain
Required not the cost, the toyle, and pain.
Full thirteen yeares in this strange work he spent,
Before he could accomplish his intent ,
And though a Victor home his Army leads,
With peeled shoulders, and with balded heads;
When in the *Tyrian* wars, the King was hot,
Jehoiakim his Oath had clean forgot ,
Thinks thus the fittest time to break his bands,
While *Babels* King thus deep ingaged stands ,
But he (alas) whose fortunes now i'th ebbe,
Had all his hopes like to a Spiders web ,
For this great King, with-drawes part of his force,
To *Judah* marches with a speedy course,

G   And

And unexpected findes the feeble Prince,
Whom he chastiled for his proud offence ;
Fast bound, intends at *Babel* he shal stay,
But chang'd his minde, and slew him by the way ;
Thus cast him out, like to a naked Asse,
For this was he, for whom none said, Alas !
His Son three months he suffered to reign,
Then from his throne, he pull'd him down again ;
Whom with his Mother, he to *Babel* led,
And more then thirty years in prison fed,
His Unckle, he establithed in's place,
Who was laft King of holy *Davids* race ;
But he, as perjur'd as *Jehoiakim*,
And th loft more (then e're they loft) by him ;
Seven years he keeps his faith, and safe he dwels,
But in the eighth, against his Prince rebels ,
The ninth, came *Nebuchadnezzar* with power,
Besieg'd his City, Temple, *Zions* Tower,
And after eighteen months he took them all,
The wals so strong, that stood so long, now fall ;
The cursed King, by flight could no wise free
His wel deserv'd, and fore-told misery ;
But being caught, to *Babels* wrathful King,
With Children, Wives, and Nobles, all they bring,
Where to the sword, all but himself was put,
And with that woful sight his eyes close shut
A haplesse man, whose darksome contemplation,
Was nothing, but such gaftly meditation ,
In midft of *Babel* now, til death he lyes,
Yet as was told, ne're saw it with his eyes ,
The Temple's burnt, the Veſſels had away,
The Towers, and Palaces, brought to decay ;

Where

Where late, of Harp, and Lute, was heard the noyse,
Now *Zim*, and *Sim*, lift up their shriking voyce;
All now of worth, are captive led with tears,
There sit bewailing *Zion* seventy years,
With all these Conquests, *Babels* King rests not,
No, nor when *Moab*, *Edom* he had got
Kedar, *Hagar*, the *Arabians* too,
All Vassals, at his hands, for grace must sue;
A totall Conquest of rich *Ægypt* makes,
All rule, he from the ancient *Pharoes* takes:
Who had for sixteen hundred years born sway,
To *Babylons* proud King, now yeelds the day.
Then *Put*, and *Lud*, doe at his mercy stand,
Where e're he goes, he Conquers every Land;
His sumptuous buildings passes all conceit,
Which wealth, and strong ambition made so great;
His Image, *Iudahs* Captives worship not,
Although the Furnace be seven times more hot;
His Dreams, wise *Daniel* doth expound ful well,
And his unhappy change with grief fore tel,
Strange melancholly humours on him lay,
Which for seven years his reason took away;
Which from no natural causes did proceed,
For by the Heavens above it was decreed:
The time expir'd, remains a Beast no more,
Resumes his Government, as heretofore.
In splender, and in Majesty, he sits,
Contemplating those times he lost his wits,
And if by words, we may guesse at the heart,
This King among the righteous had a part:
Forty four years he reign'd, which being run,
He left his Wealth, and Conquest, to his Son.

Ealme

Evilmerodach.

*B*Abels great Monarch, now laid in the dust,
His son possesses wealth, and rule, as just;
    And in the first year of his royalty,
Easeth *Jehoiakims* captivity.
Poor forlorn Prince, that had all state forgot,
In seven and thirty years, had seen no jot,
Among the Conquered Kings, that there did lye,
Is *Judah's* King, now lifted up on high
But yet in *Babell*, he must still remain:
And native *Canaan*, never see again,
Unlike his father, *Evilmerodach*,
Prudence, and magnanimity, did lack
Faire *Ægypt* is, by his remisseneße lost;
Arabia, and all the boardering coast
Wars with the *Medes*, unhappily he wag'd,
(Within which broiles, rich *Cræsus* was engag'd,)
His Army routed, and himselfe there slain,
His Kingdome to *Belshazzar* did remain.

Belshazzar.

*U*Nworthy *Belshazzar* next weares the Crown,
Whose prophane acts, a sacred pen sets down.
    His lust, and cruelty, in books we find,
A Royall State, rul'd by a bruitish mind
His life so base, and dissolute, invites
The Noble *Persius*, to invade his rights.

Who

Who with his own, and Uncles power anon;
Layes siedge to's regall seat, proud *Babylon*,
The coward King, whose strength lay in his walls;
To banquetting, and revelling now falls,
To shew his little dread, but greater store,
To chear his friends, and scorn his foes the more.
The holy vessells, thither brought long since,
Carous'd they in, and sacrilegious Prince,
Did praise his gods of mettall, wood, and stone,
Protectors of his Crown, and *Babylon*,
But he above, his doings did deride,
And with a hand, soon dashed all his pride.
The King, upon the wall casting his eye,
The fingers of his hand-writing did spy.
Which horrid sight, he fears, must needs portend,
Destruction to his Crown, to's Person end.
With quaking knees, and heart appall'd, he crys,
For the Soothsayers, and Magicians wise,
This language strange, to read, and to unfold,
With guifts of Scarlet robe, and Chaines of gold,
And highest dignity, next to the King,
To him that could interpret clear this thing:
But dumb the gazing Astrologers stand,
Amazed at the writing, and the hand.
None answers the affrighted Kings intent.
Who still expects some fearfull sad event,
As thus amort he sits, as all undone.
In comes the Queen, to chear her heartlesse son.
Of *Daniel* tells, who in his Grand sires dayes,
Was held in more request, then now he was,
Daniel in haste, is brought before the King,
Who doth not flatter, nor once cloake the thing

G 3

Re-minds him of his Grand—sires height, and fall,
And of his own notorious sins, withall ;
His drunkennesse, and his prophainnesse high,
His pride, and sottish grosse Idolatry.
The guilty King, with colour pale, and dead,
There hears his *Mene*, and his *Tekel* read ,
And did one thing worthy a King (though late)
Perform'd his word, to him, that told his fate ;
That night victorious *Cyrus* took the town,
Who soone did terminate his Life, and Crown :
With him did end the race of *Baludan*,
And now the *Persian* Monarchy began.

The end of the Assyrian Monarchy.

The

The Second Monarchy,

being the *Perſian,* begun under
Cyrus, Darius (being his Vnckle,
and his Father in Law) reign-
ing with him about two years.

Yrus Cambyſes, Son of *Perſia's* King,
Whom Lady *Mandana* did to him bring,
She Daughter unto great *Aſtiages,*
He in deſcent the ſeventh from *Arbaces*
Cambyſes was of *Achemenes* race,
Who had in *Perſia* the Lieutenants place.
When *Sardanapalus* was over-thrown,
And from that time, had held it as his own ;
Cyrus, Darius Daughter took to wife,
And ſo unites two Kingdoms, without ſtrife ;
Darius was unto *Mandana* brother,
Adopts her Son for his, having no other :
This is of *Cyrus* the true pedigree,
Whoſe Anceſtors, were royal in degree ;
His Mothers Dream, and Grand-ſires cruelty,
His preſervation in his miſery,
His nouriſhment aſforded by a Bitch,
Are ſit for ſuch, whoſe cares tor ſables rich,

He in his younger dayes an Army led,
Against great *Cressus*, then of *Lidia* head;
Who over-curious of wars event,
For information to *Apollo* went:
And the ambiguous Oracle did trust,
So over-thrown of *Gyrus*, as was just,
Who him pursues to *Sardis*, takes the town,
Where all that doe resist, are slaughter'd down;
D'sguised *Cressus*, hop'd to scape i'th throng,
Who had no might to save himself from wrong;
But as he past, his Son, who was born dumbe,
With pressing grief, and sorrow, over-come,
Amidst the tumult, bloud shed, and the strife,
Brake his long silence, cry'd, spare *Cressus* life:
Cressus thus known, it was great *Cyrus* doome,
(A hard decree) to ashes he consume;
Then on a Pike being set, where all might eye,
He *Solon, Solon, Solor*, thrice did cry.
Upon demand, his minde to *Cyrus* broke,
And told, how *So'on* in his hight had spoke.
With pitty *Cyrus* mov'd, knowing Kings stand,
Now up, now down, as fortune turnes her hand,
Weighing the age, and greatnesse of the Prince,
(His Mothers Vnckle, stories doe evince.)
Gave him at once, his life, and Kingdom too,
And with the *Lidians*, had no more to doe.
Next war, the restlesse *Cyrus* thought upon,
Was conquest of the stately *Babylon*,
Now trebble wall'd, and moated so about,
That all the world they neither feare, nor doubt,
To draw this ditch, he many sluces cut,
But till convenient time their heads kept shut;

                                                      Tha:

That night *Belshazzar* feasted all his rout,
He cuts those banks, and let the river out,
And to the walls securely marches on,
Not finding a defendant thereupon;
Enters the town, the sottish King he slayes,
Upon earths richest spoyles his Souldiers preys;
Here twenty yeares provision he found,
Forty five mile this City scarce could round;
This head of Kingdoms, *Caldes* excellence,
For Owles, and Satyres, makes a residence,
Yet wondrous Monuments this stately Queen,
Hid after thousand yeares faire to be seen
Cyrus doth now the *Jewish* captives free,
An Edict makes, the Temple builded be,
He with his Vnckle *Daniel* sets on high,
And caus'd his foes in Lions den to dye
Long after this, he 'gainst the *Sythians* goes,
And *Tomris* Son, an Army over-throwes,
Which to revenge, she hires a mighty power,
And sets on *Cyrus*, in a fatall houre,
There routs his Hoast, himself she prisoner takes,
And at one blow, wor'ds head, she headlesse makes;
The which she bak'd within a Bat of bloud,
Vsing such taunting words as she thought good.
But *Zenophon* reports, he dy'd in's bed,
In honour, peace, and wealth, with a grey head,
And in his Town of *Pasargida* lyes,
Where *Alexander* sought, in hope of prize,
But in this Tombe was only to be found
Two *Sythian* bowes, a sword, and target round,
Where that proud Conquerour could doe no lesse,
Then at his Herse great honours to expresse,

Three

Three Daughters, and two Sons, he left behind,
Innobled more by birth, then by their mind ;
Some thirty years this potent Prince did reign,
Unto *Cambyses* then, all did remain.

Cambyses.

Cambyses, no wayes like, his noble Sire,
But to enlarge his state, had some desire ,
His reign with Bloud, and Incest, first begins,
Then tends to finde a Law for these his sins ;
That Kings with Sisters match, no Law they finde,
But that the *Persian* King, may act his minde ,
Which Law includes all Lawes, though lawlesse stil,
And makes it lawful Law, if he but wil ,
He wages warre, the fifth year of his reign,
'Gainst *Ægypts* King, who there by him was slain,
And all of Royal bloud that came to hand,
He seized first of life, and then of Land ,
(But little *Myrus*, scap'd that cruel fate,
Who grown a man, resum'd again his state)
He next to *Cyprus* sends his bloudy Hoast,
Who landed soon upon that fruitful coast,
Made *Evelthon* their King, with bended knee,
To hold his own, of his free courtesie ,
The Temples he destroyes not, for his zeal,
But he would be profest god of their Weal ,
Yea, in his pride, he ventured so farre,
To spoyl the Temple of great *Jupiter*,
But as they marched o're those desart sands,
The stormed dust o're-whelm'd his during bands,

P.ut

But scorning thus by *Jove* to be out-brav'd,
A second Army there had almost grav'd;
But vain he found, to fight with Elements,
So left his sacrilegious bold intents.
The Ægyptian *Apis* then he likewise slew,
Laughing to scorn that calvish, sottish crew.
If all his heat, had been for a good end,
Cambyses to the clouds, we might commend,
But he that 'fore the gods, himself preferrs,
Is more prophane, then grosse Idolaters;
And though no gods, if he esteem them some,
And contemn them, woful is his doome.
He after this, saw in a Vision,
His brother *Smerdis* sit upon his throne;
He strait to rid himself of causlesse fears,
Complots the Princes death, in his green years,
Who for no wrong, poore innocent must dye,
Praxaspes now must act this tragedy,
Who into *Persia* with Commission sent,
Accomplished this wicked Kings intent;
His sister, whom incestuously he wed,
Hearing her harmlesse brother thus was dead,
His woful fate with tears did so bemoane,
That by her Husbands charge, she caught her owne;
She with her fruit was both at once undone,
Who would have born a Nephew, and a Son.
O hellish Husband, Brother, Vnckle, Sire,
Thy cruelty will Ages still admire.
This strange severity, one time he us'd,
Upon a Judge, for breach of Law accus'd,
Flayd him alive, hung up his stuffed skin
Over his Seat, then plac'd his Son therein;

To

To whom he gave this in rememberance,
Like fault must look, for the like recompence,
Praraspes, to *Cambyses* favourite,
Having one son, in whom he did delight,
His cruell Master, for all service done,
Shot through the heart of his beloved son:
And only for his fathers faithfullnesse,
Who said but what, the King bad him expresse.
'T would be no pleasant, but a tedious thing,
To tell the facts, of this most bloody King
Fear'd of all, but lov'd of few, or none,
All thought his short raign long, till it was done.
At last, two of his Officers he hears,
Had set a *Smerdis* up, of the same years;
And like in feature, to the *Smerdis* dead,
Ruling as they thought good, under his head.
Toucht with this newes, to *Persia* he makes,
But in the way, his sword just vengeance takes.
Unsheathes, as he his horse mounted on high,
And with a *Martall* thrust, wounds him ith' thigh,
Which ends before begun, the *Persian* Warre,
Yeelding to death, that dreadfull Conquerer.
Grefe for his brothers death, he did expresse,
And more, because he dyed issulesse.
The Male line, of great *Cyrus* now did end.
The Female many ages did extend,
A *Babylon* in *Egypt* did he make
And built fair *Meroe*, for his sisters sake.
Eight years he reign'd, a short, yet too long time,
Cut off in's wickednesse, in's strength, and prime.

The

The *inter Regnum between* Cambyses, *and* Darius Hyslaspes.

CHildlesse *Cambyses,* on the sudden dead,
The Princes meet to chuse one in his stead,
Of which the cheife were seven, call'd *Satrapes,*
(Who like to Kings, rul'd Kingdomes as they please,)
Descended all, of *Achimenes* blood,
And kinsmen in account, to th' King they stood,
And first these noble *Magi* 'gree upon,
To thrust th' Imposter *Smerdis* out of throne,
Their Forces instantly they raise, and rout,
This King, with conspirators so stout,
Who little pleasure had, in his short reigne,
And now with his accomplyces lye slaine.
But yet, 'fore this was done, much blood was shed,
And two of these great Peers, in place lay dead:
Some write that sorely hurt, they 'scap'd away,
But so or no, sure tis, they won the day.
All things in peace, and Rebells throughly quel'd,
A Consultation by the States was held.
What forme of Government now to erect,
The old, or new, which best, in what respect,
The greater part, declin'd a Monarchy.
So late crusht by their Princes Tyranny;
And thought the people, would more happy be,
If governed by an Aristocracy.
But others thought (none of the dullest braine,)
But better one, then many Tyrants reigne.
What arguments they us'd, I know not well,
Too politicke (tis like) for me to tell,

But

But in conclusion they all agree,
That of the seven a Monarch chosen be ;
All envie to avoyd, this was thought on,
Upon a Green to meet, by rising Sun ;
And he whose Horse before the rest should neigh,
Of all the Peers should have precedency.
They all attend on the appointed houre,
Praying to Fortune, for a Kingly power ;
Then mounting on their snorting coursers proud;
Darius lusty stallion neighed full loud ;
The Nobles all alight, their King to greet,
And after *Persian* manner, kisse his feet.
His happy wishes now doth no man spare,
But acclamations ecchoes in the aire ,
A thousand times, God save the King, they cry,
Let tyranny now with *Cambyses* dye.
They then attend him, to his royall roome,
Thanks for all this to's crafty Stable-groome.

Darius Hystaspes.

Darius by election made a King,
His title to make strong omits nothing ;
He two of *Cyrus* Daughters now doth wed,
Two of his Neeces takes to nuptiall bed ;
By which he cuts their hopes (for future times)
That by such steps to Kingdoms often climbs.
And a w a King, by marriage, choyce, and bloud,
Three strings to's bow, the least of which is good ;
Yet more the peoples hearts firmly to binde,
Made wholsome gentle Laws, which pleas'd each mind

His

His affability, and milde aspect,
Did win him loyalty, and all respect;
Yet notwithstanding he did all so well,
The *Babylonians* 'gainst their Prince rebell;
An Hoast he rais'd, the City to reduce,
But strength against those walls was of no use,
For twice ten months before the town he lay,
And fear'd, he now with scorn must march away:
Then brave *Zopirus*, for his Masters good,
His manly face dis-figures, spares no bloud,
With his own hands cuts off his eares, and nose,
And with a faithfull fraud to'th' town he goes,
Tels them, how harshly the proud King had dealt,
That for their sakes, his cruelty he felt;
Desiring of the Prince to raise the siege,
This violence was done him by his Leige,
This told, for enterance he stood not long,
For they beleev'd his nose, more then his tongue;
With all the Cities strength they him betrust,
If he command, obey the greatest must:
When opportunity he saw was fit,
Delivers up the town, and all in it.
To loose a nose, to win a Town's no shame,
But who dare venture such a stake for th' game,
Then thy disgrace, thine honour's manifold,
Who doth deserve a Statue made of gold,
Nor can *Persia* in his Monarchy,
Scarse finde enough to thank thy loyalty,
But yet thou hast sufficient recompence,
In that thy fame shall sound whilst men have sence,
Yet o're thy glory we must cast this vaile,
Thy falshood, not thy valour did prevaile,

Thy

Thy wit was more then was thine honesty,
Thou lov'dst thy Master more then verity.
Darius in the second of his reign,
An Edict for the *Jews* publish'd again,
The temple to re-build, for that did rest
Since *Cyrus* time, *Cambyses* did molest ;
He like a King, now grants a Charter large,
Out of his owne revenues beares the charge ;
Gives sacrifices, wheat, wine, oyle, and salt,
Threats punishment to him, that through default
Shall let the work, or keep back any thing,
Of what is freely granted by the King,
And on all Kings he poures out execrations,
That shall, but dare rize those firme foundations;
They thus backt of the King, in spight of foes,
Built on, and prosper'd, till their walls did close ;
And in the sixth veare of his friendly reign
Set up a Temple (though, a lesse)again.
Darius on the *Sythians* made a war,
Entring that large and barren country far,
A bridge he made, which serv'd for boat, and barge,
Over fair *Ister*, at a mighty charge ;
But in that Desart, 'mongst his barbarous foes,
Sharp wants, not swords, his vallour did oppose,
His Army fought with Hunger, and with Cold,
Which two then to assaile, his Camp was bold :
By these alone his Hoast was pinch'd so sore,
He warr'd defensive, not offensive, more,
The Salvages did laugh at his distresse,
Their minds by Hieroglyphicks they expresse;
A Frog, a Mouse, a Bird, an Arrow sent,
The King will needs interpret their intent,

Posses-

Poffeffion of water, earth, and aire,
But wife *Gobrias* reads not half fo farre :
Quoth he, like *Frogs*, in water we muft dive,
Or like to Mice, under the earth muft live ;
Or fly like birds, in unknown wayes full quick;
Or *Sythian* arrows in our fides muft ftick
The King, feeing his men, and victuall fpent,
His fruitleffe war, began late to repent ;
Return'd with little honour, and leffe gaine,
His enemies fcarce feen, then much leffe, flaine;
He after this, intends *Greece* to invade,
But troubles in leffe *Afia* him ftay'd ,
Which hufht, he ftraight fo orders his affaires;
For *Attica* an Army he prepares ,
But as before, fo now with ill fucceffe,
Return'd with wondrous loffe, and honour leffe:
Athens perceiving now their defperate ftate,
Arm'd all they could, which elev'n thoufand make ;
By brave *Miltiades* (their chief) being led,
Darius multitude befoe them fled ,
At *Marathon* this bloudy field was fought,
Where *Grecians* prov'd themfelves right *Souldiers,*
The *Perfians* to their Gallies poft with fpeed, (ftour;
Where an *Athenian* fhew'd a valiant deed,
Purfues his flying-foes, and on the ftrand,
He ftayes a landing Gally with his hand ,
Which foon cut eft, he with the left
Renews his hold , but when of that bereft,
His whetted teeth he fticks in the firm wood,
Of flyes his head, down fhowres his frolick blood
So t *erfians* carry home that angry peece,
As the beft trophe that they won in *Greece*

Darius light, he heavie, home returnes,
And for revenge his heart still restlesse burnes ,
His Queen *Attossa*, caused all this stir,
For *Grecian* Maids ('tis said) to wait on her ;
She lost her aimes, her Husband, he lost more,
His men, his coyn, his honour, and his store ,
And the ensuing yeare ended his life,
('Tis thought) through grief of his successlesse strife,
Thirty six years this royall Prince did reign,
Unto his eldest Son, all did remain.

Xerxes.

XErxes, *Darius*, and *Attossa*'s Son,
  Grand-childe to *Cyrus*, now sits on the throne ;
  The Father not so full of lenity,
As is the Son, of pride, and cruelty ,
He with his Crown, receives a double warre,
Th' *Ægiptians* to reduce, and *Greece* to marre ;
The first begun, and finish'd in such hast,
None write by whom, nor how, 'twas over past ;
But for the last he made such preparation,
As if to dust he meant to grinde that Nation,
Yet all his men, and instruments of slaughter,
Produced but derision, and laughter ,
Sage *Artabanus* counsell, had he taken,
And's cousen, young *Mardonius* forsaken,
His Souldiers, credit, wealth, at home had stay'd,
And *Greece* such wondrous triumphs ne're had made.
The first deports, and layes before his eyes,
His Father's ill successe in's enterprise,

Aguiſt

Against the Sythians, and *Grecians* too,
What infamy to's honour did accrue.
Flattering *Mardonius* on th' other side,
With certainty of *Europe* feeds his pride;
Vaine *Xerxes* thinks his counsell hath most wit,
That his ambitious humour best can fit,
And by this choyce, unwarily posts on,
To present losse, future subversion;
Although he hasted, yet foure yeares was spent,
In great provisions, for this great intent,
His Army of all Nations, was compounded,
That the large *Persian* government surrounded,
His Foot was seventeen hundred thousand strong,
Eight hundred thousand Horse to them belong,
His Camels, beasts, for carriage numberlesse,
For truth's asham'd how many to expresse,
The charge of all he severally commended,
To Princes of the *Persian* bloud descended,
But the command of these Commanders all,
To *Mardonius*, Captain Generall,
He was the Son of the fore-nam'd *Gobrias*,
Who married the sister of *Darius*
These his Land Forces were, then next, a Fleet
Of two and twenty thousand Gallies meet,
Mann'd by *Phenisians*, and *Pamphilians*,
Cipriots, *Dorians*, and *Cilicians*,
Lycians, *Carians*, and *Ionians*,
Æolians, and the *Hellespontines*,
Besides, the Vessels for his transportation,
Three thousand (or more) by best relation,
Artemesia, *Halicarna's* Queene,
In person there, now for his help was seen,

H 2 *Whose*

Whose Gallies all the rest in'neatnesse passe,
Save the *Zidonians*, where *Xerxes* was
Hers she kept stil, seperate from the rest,
For to command alone, she thought was best
O noble Queen, thy valour I commend,
But pitty 'twas, thine ayde that here did'st lend,
At *Sardis*, in *Lidia*, these all doe meet,
Whither rich *Pithius* comes, *Xerxes* to greet,
Feasts all this multitude, of his own charge,
Then gives the King, a King-like gift, most large;
Three thousand Tallents of the purest gold,
Which mighty sum, all wondred to behold.
He humbly to the King then makes request,
One of his five Sons there, might be relea'd,
To be to's age a comfort, and a stay,
The other four he freely gave away:
The King cals for the Youth, who being brought,
Cuts him in twain, for whom hisSire besought.
O most inhumain incivility!
Nay, more then monstrous barb'rous cruelty
For his great love, is this thy recompence?
Is this to doe like *Xerxes*, or a Prince
Thou shame of Kings, of men the detestation,
I Rhethorick want, to poure out execration:
First thing, *Xerxes* did worthy recount,
A Sea passage cuts, behind *Orthos* Mount.
Next, o're the *Hellespont* a bridge he made,
Of Boats, together coupled, and there laid;
But winds, and waves, these couples soon dissever'd,
Yet *Xerxes* in his, enterprise, persever'd,
Seven thousand Gallies chain'd, by *Tyrians* skill,
I amly at length, accomplished his wil,

Seven dayes and nights, his Hoast without least stay,
Was marching o're this interrupting Bay;
And in *Abidus* Plaines, mustring his Forces,
He glories in his Squadrons, and his Horses,
Long viewing them, thought it great happinesse,
One King, so many Subjects should possesse,
But yet this goodly sight produced teares,
That none of these should live a hundred yeares:
What after did ensue, had he fore seen,
Of so long time, his thoughts had never been
Of *Artabanus* he again demands,
How of this enterprise his thoughts now stands,
His answer was, both Land and Sea he feared,
Which was not vaine, as it soon appeared:
But *Xerxes* resolute, to *Thrace* goes first,
His Hoast, who *Lissus* drinks to quench their thirst,
And for his Cattell, all *Pissirus* Lake
Was scarce enough, for each a draught to take.
Then marching to the streight *Thermopyle*,
The *Spartan* meets him, brave *Leonide*,
This 'twixt the Mountains lyes (half Acre wide)
That pleasant *Thessaly*, from *Greece* divide,
Two dayes and nights a fight they there maintain,
Till twenty thousand *Persians* falls down slain,
And all that Army, then dismay'd, had fled,
But that a Fugative discovered,
How part might o're the Mountains goe about,
And wound the backs of those bold Warriours stout.
They thus behemm'd with multitude of foes,
Laid on more fiercely, their deep mortall blowes,
None cryes for quarter, nor yet seeks to run,
But on their ground they dye, each Mothers Son.

O noble *Greeks*, how now, degenerate ?
Where is the valour, of your antient State ?
When as one thousand, could some Millions daunt,
Alas, it is *Leonides* you want !
This shamefull Victory cost *Xerxes* deare,
Amongst the rest, two brothers he lost there ;
And as at Land, so he at Sea was crost,
Four hundred stately Ships by stormes was lost,
Of Vessels small almost innumerable,
Them to receive, the Harbour was not able ,
Yet thinking to out match his foes at Sea,
Inclos'd their Fleet i'th' streights of *Eubea* ;
But they as valiant by Sea, as Land,
In this Streight, as the other, firmly stand
And *Xerxes* mighty Gallies batter'd so,
That their split sides, witness'd his overthrow ;
Yet in the Streights of *Salamis* he try'd,
If that smal number his great force could bide ,
But he, in daring of his forward foe,
Received there, a shameful over throw.
Twice beaten thus by Sea, he warr'd no more
But *Phocæus* Land, he then wasted sore
They no way able to withstand his force,
That brave *Thymistocles* takes this wise course,
In secret manner word to *Xerxes* sends,
That *Greeks* to break his bridge shortly intends ,
And as a friend, warns him, what e're he doe,
For his retreat, to have an eye thereto .
He hearing this, his thoughts, and course home bend,
Much, that which never was intended !
Yet 'fore he went, to help out his expence,
Part of his Hoast to *Delphos* sent from thence,

To rob the wealthy Temple of *Apollo*,
But mischief, Sacriledge, doth ever follow,
Two mighty Rocks, brake from *Parnassus* Hil,
And many thousands of these men did kil,
Which accident, the rest affrighted so,
With empty hands they to their Master go;
He seeing all thus tend unto decay,
Thought it his best, no longer for to stay,
Three hundred thousand yet he left behind,
With his *Mardon'us*, judex of his minde,
Who for his sake, he knew, would venture far,
(Chief instigater of this hopelesse War;)
He instantly to *Athens* sends for peace,
That all Hostility might thence-forth cease,
And that with *Xerxes* they would be at one,
So should all favour to their State be shown.
The *Spartans*, fearing *Athens* would agree,
As had *Macedon*, *Thebes*, and *Thessalie*,
And leave them out, the shock for to sustaine,
By their Ambassador they thus complain,
That *Xerxes* quarrel was 'gainst *Athens* State,
And they had helpt them, as confederate,
If now in need, they should thus fail their friends,
Their infamy would last til all things ends.
But the *Athenians*, this peace detest,
And thus reply'd unto *Mardon's* request,
That whilst the Sun did run his endlesse course,
Against the *Persians* they would use their force.
Nor could the brave Ambassador be sent,
With Rhetorick, t' gain better complement.
Though of this Nation borne a great Commander,
No lesse then Grand-sire to great *Alexander*.

Mardonius proud, hearing this answer stout,
To adde unto his numbers, layes about,
And of those *Greeks*, which by his skil he'd won,
He fifty thousand joynes unto his own ,
The other *Greeks*, which were confederate,
One hundred thousand, and ten thousand make.
The *Beotian* fields, of war, the seats,
Where both sides exercis'd their manly feats ,
But all their controversies to decide,
For one maine Battell shortly, both provide ,
The *Athenians* could but forty thousand arme,
For other Weapons, they had none would harme ,
But that which helpt defects, and made them bold,
Was victory, by Oracle fore-told .
Ten dayes these Armies did each other see,
Mardonius finding victuals wast apace,
No longer dar'd, but fiercely on-set gave,
The other not a hand, nor sword will wave,
Till in the entrails of their Sacrifice,
The signall of their victory doth rise,
Which found, like *Greeks* they fight, the *Persians* fl,
And troublesome *Mardonius* now must dye
All's lost, and of three hundred thousand men,
Three thousand scapes, for to run home agen ,
For pitty, let those few to *Xerxes* go,
To certifie this finall over throw
Same day, the small remainder of his Fleet,
The *Grecians* at *Mycale* in *Asia* meet,
And here so utterly they wrack d the same,
Scarce one was left, to carry home the same ,
This did the *Greeks* destroy, consume, displace,
That Army, which did fright the Universe,

Scorn'd *Xerxes*, hated for his cruelty.
Yet ceases not to act his villany:
His brother's wife, sollicites to his will;
The chaste, and beautious *Dime*, refuses still.
Some years by him in this vain suit was spent,
Yet words, nor guifts, could win him least content:
Nor matching of her daughter, to his son :
But she was stil, as when it first begun.
When jealous Queen *Amestris*, of this knew,
She *Harpy*-like, upon the Lady flew:
Cut off her lilly breasts, her nose, and ears;
And leaves her thus, besmear'd with blood, and tears:
Straight comes her Lord,   and finds his wife thus lie,
The sorrow of his heart, did close his eye :
He dying to behold, that wounding sight,
Where he had sometime gaz'd with great delight.
To see that face, where Rose and Lilly stood,
O're-flown with torrent of her ruby blood.
To see those breasts, where chastity did dwel,
Thus cut, and mangled by a hag of hell
With loaden heart unto the King he goes,
Tels as he could, his unexpress'd woes,
But for his deep complaints, and showres of tears,
His brothers recompence was naught but jears.
The grieved Prince finding nor right, nor love,
To *Bactria* his houshold did remove
His wicked brother, after sent a crew,
Which him, and his, most barbrously there slew,
Unto such height did grow his cruelty,
Of life, no man had least security.
At last his Uncle, did his death conspire,
And for that end, his Eunuch he did hire.

Which

Which wretch, him privately smother'd in's bed,
But yet by search, he was found murthered,
The *Artacanus* hirer of this deed,
That from suspition he might be freed,
Accus'd *Darius*, *Xerx's* eldest son,
To be the Authour of the deed was done,
And by his craft, order'd the matter so,
That the poor innocent, to death must go
But in short time, this wickednesse was knowne,
For which he dyed, and not he alone.
But all his family was likewise slain,
Such Justice then, in *Persia* did remain,
The eldest son, thus immaturely dead,
The second was inthron'd, in's fathers stead

Artaxerxes Longimanus.

Amongst the Monarchs next, this Prince had place
The best that ever sprang of *Cyrus* race.
He first, war with revolting *Ægypt* made
To whom the perjur'd *Grecians* lent their aide,
Although to *Xerxes*, they not long before,
A league of amity, had sworn before
Which had they kept, *Greece* had more nobly done,
Then when the world, they after over-run.
Greeks and *Egyptians* both, he overthrows,
And payes them now, according as he owes,
Which done, a sumptuous feast, makes like a King
Where ninescore dayes, are spent in banquetting,
His Princes, Nobles, and his Captaines calls,
To be partakers in these festivals.

H s

His hangings, white, and green, and purple dye,
With gold and silver beds, most gorgiously.
The royall wine, in golden cups doth passe,
To drink more then he list, none bidden was.
Queen *Vashty* also feasts, but 'fore tis ended,
Alas, she from her Royalty's suspended.
And a more worthy, placed in her roome,
By *Memucan's* advice, this was the doome.
What *Hester* was, and did, her story reed,
And how her Country-men from spoile she freed.
Of *Hamans* fall, and *Mordica's* great rise,
The might o'th' Prince, the tribute on the Isles.
Unto this King *Thymistocles* did flye,
When under *Ostracisme* he did lye
For such ingratitude, did *Athens* show
This valiant Knight, whom they so much did owe,
Such entertainment with this Prince he found,
That in all Loyalty his heart was bound,
The King not little joyfull of this chance,
Thinking his *Grecian* wars new to advance.
And for that end, great preparation made,
Fair *Attica*, a third time to invade
His Grand sires old disgrace, did vex him sore,
His father *Xerxes* losse, and shame, much more,
For punishment, their breach of oath did call,
The noble *Greek*, now fit for generall.
Who for his wrong, he could not chuse but deem,
His Country, nor his Kindred would esteem,
Provisions, and season now being fit,
T'*Thymistocles* he doth his war commit,
But he all injury, had soon forgate,
And to his Country-men could bear no hate.

Nor yet disloyall to his Prince would prove,
To whom oblig'd, by favour, and by love,
Either to wrong, did wound his heart so sore,
To wrong himselfe by death, he chose before:
In this sad conflict, marching on his ways,
Strong peyson took, and put an end to's dayes.
The King this noble Captaine having lost,
Again dispersed, his new levyed hoast
Rest of his time in peace he did remain,
And dy'd the two and fortieth of his reign.

Daryus Nothus.

Three sons great *Artaxerxes* left behind;
The eldest to succeed, that was his mind.
But he, with his next brother fell at strife,
That nought appeas'd him, but his brothers life.
Then the surviver is by *Nothus* slaine,
Who now sole Monarch, doth of all remaine,
These two lewd sons, are by hystorians thought,
To be by *Hester*, to her husband brought.
If they were hers, the greater was her mown,
That for such gracelesse wretches she did groan,
Disquiet *Egypt*, 'gainst this King rebells,
Drives out his garison that therein dwels.
Joynes with the *Greeks*, and so maintains their right,
For sixty years maugre the *Persians* might.
A second trouble, after this succee's
Which from remissenesse, in *Asia* proceeds
Amorges, whom their Vice-roy he ordain'd
Revolts, having treasure, and people gain'd

In-

Invades the Country, and much trouble wrought,
Before to quietnesse things could be brought,
The King was glad, with *Sparta* to make peace,
So that he might, these tumults soon appease.
But they in *Asia*, must first restore
All Townes, held by his Ancestors before.
The King much profit reapeth, by these leagues,
Re-gaines his own, and then the Rebell breaks:
Whose forces by their helpe were overthrown,
And so each man again possest his owne.
The King, his sister, like *Cambyses*, wed;
More by his pride, then lust, thereunto led.
(For *Persian* Kings, did deem themselves so good,
No match was high enough, but their own blood,)
Two sons she bore, the youngest *Cyrus* nam'd,
A hopefull Prince, whose worth is ever fam'd.
His father would no notice of that take;
Prefers his brother, for his birth-rights sake.
But *Cyrus* scornes, his brothers feeble wit,
And takes more on him, then was judged fit.
The King provok'd, sends for him to the Court,
Meaning to chastise him, in sharpest sort,
But in his slow approach, ere he came there,
His fathers death, did put an end to's fear.
Nothus reign'd nineteen years, which run,
His large Dominions left, to's eldest son.

Artaxerxes Mnemon.

MNemon now sits upon his fathers Throne,
Yet doubts, all he injoyes, is not his own,

Still on his brother, casts a jealous eye,
Judging all's actions, tends to's injury.
Cyrus o'th' other side, weighs in his mind,
What helps, in's enterprize he's like to find,
His interest, in the Kingdome, now next heir,
More deare to's mother, then his brother far.
His brothers litle love, like to be gone,
Held by his mothers intercession.
These and like motives, hurry him amain,
To win by force, what right could not obtain.
And thought it best, now in his mothers time,
By lesser steps, towards the top to climbe,
If in his enterprize he should fall short,
She to the King, would make a fair report.
He hop'd, if fraud, nor force the Crown could gaine;
Her prevailence, a pardon might obtain.
From the Lieutenant first, he takes away,
Some Townes commodious in lesse *Asia,*
Pretending still, the profit of the King,
Whose rents and customes, duly he sent in.
The King finding, revenues now amended,
For what was done, seemed no whit offended.
Then next, the *Lacedemons* he takes to pay,
(One *Greeke* could make ten *Persians* run away)
Great care was his pretence, those Souldiers stour,
The Rovers in *Pisidia,* should drive out.
But least some worser newes should fly to Court,
He meant himselfe to carry the report
And for that end, five hundred Horse he chose,
With posting speed towards the King he goes,
But fame more quick, arrives ere he came there,
And fills the Court with tumult, and with fear.

The

The young Queen, and old, at bitter jars.
The one accus'd the other, for these wars ·
The wife, against the mother, still doth cry
To be the Author of conspiracy
The King dismay'd, a mighty Hoast doth raise,
Which Cyrus heares, and so fore slowes his pace ·
But as he goes, his Forces still augmen's,
Seven hundred Greeks now further his intents
And others to be warm'd by this new sun,
In numbers from his brother daily run.
The fearfull King, at last, musters his Forces,
And counts nine hundred thousand foot and horses:
And yet with these, had neither heart, nor grace,
To look his manly brother in the face.
Three hundred thousand, yet to Syria sent;
To keep those streights, to hinder his intent
Their Captain hearing, but of Cyrus name,
Ran back, and quite abandoned the same,
Abrocomes, was this base cowards name,
Not worthy to be known, but for his shame,
This place was made, by nature, and by art,
Few might have kept it, had they but a heart
Cyrus dispair'd, a passage there to gain,
So hir'd a fleet, to wast him ore the Maine,
The mazed King, was now about to fly;
To th' utmost parts of Baby's, and there lye.
Had not a Captain, sore against his will,
By reason, and by force, detain'd him still
Up then with speed, a mighty trench he threwes,
For his security, against his foes
Six yards the depth, and forty miles the length,
Some fifty, or else sixty foote in breadth

Yet

Yet for his brothers comming, durst not stay,
He surest was, when furthest out o' th' way.
Cyrus finding his campe, and no man there;
Rejoyced not a little at his feare
On this, he and his souldiers cirel.sse grow,
And here,and there, in circts their Armes they throw,
When suddenly their Scouts come in and cry,
Arme,arme, the King is now app oaching nigh,
In this confusion, each man as he might,
Gets on his armes, prayes himselfe for fight,
And ranged stood, by great *Euprats* side,
The brunt of that huge multitude to bide
Of whose great numbers, their intelligence,
Was gather'd by the dust that rose from thence .
Which like a mighty cloud darkned the skye,
And black and blacker grew, as they drew nigh
But when their order, and silence they saw,
That,more then multitudes, their hearts did awe:
For tumult and confusion they expected,
And all good discipline to be neglected
But long under their fears, they did not stay,
For at first charge the *Persians* ran away.
Which did such courage to the *Grecians* bring,
They straight adored *Cyrus* for their King,
So had he been, and got the victory,
Had not his too much valour put him by.
He with six hundred, on a squadron set,
Of six thousand, wherein the King was yet,
And brought his Sou'diers on so gallantly,
They were about to leave their King and fly,
Whom *Cyrus* spi'd, cries out, I see the man,
And with a full career, at him he ran.

But

But in his speed a Dart hit him i'th' eye,
Down *Cyrus* fals, and yeilds to destiny,
His Host in chase, knowes not of his disaster,
But treads down all, for to advance their Master;
At last his head they spy upon a Launce,
Who knowes the sudden change made by this chance;
Senceleffe and mute they stand, yet breath out groans,
Nor *Gorgons* like to this, transform'd to stones.
After this trance, revenge, new spirits blew,
And now more eagerly their foes pursue,
And heaps on heaps, such multitudes they la'd,
Their armes grew weake, through slaughters that they
The King unto a country Village flyes,   (made.
And for a while unkingly there he lyes;
At last, displayes his Ensigne on a Hil,
Hoping with that to make the *Greeks* stand stil,
But was deceiv'd, to it they make amain,
The King upon the spur, runs back again,
But they too faint, still to pursue their game,
Being Victors oft, now to their Camp they came;
Nor lackt they any of their number small,
Nor wound receiv'd, but one among them all.
The King with his dispers'd also incampt
With infamy upon each fore-head stampt;
After a while his thoughts he re-collects,
Of this dayes cowardize, he feares the effects,
If *Greeks* unto their Country men declare,
What daftards in the field the *Perfians* are,
They soone may come, and place one in his Throne,
And rob him both of Scepter, and of Crown;
That their return be stopt, he judg'd was best,
That so *Europians* might no more moleft,

I   *Forth*

Forth-with he sends to's Tent, they straight addresse,
And there all wait his mercy, weaponlesse,
The *Greeks* with scorn reject his proud commands;
Asking no favour, where they fear'd no bands.
The troubled King, his Herauld sends again,
And sues for peace, that they his friends remain;
The smiling *Greeks* reply, they first must bait,
They were too hungry to capitulate;
The King great store of all provision sends,
And courtesie to th' utmost he pretends,
Such terrour on the *Persians* then did fall,
They quak'd, to heare them, to each other call
The King's perplext, here dares not let them stay,
And feares as much to let them march away,
But Kings ne're want such as can serve their will,
Fit instruments t' accomplish what is ill,
As *Tyssaphern*, knowing his Masters minde,
Invites their chief Commander, as most kinde;
And with all Oathes, and deepest flattery,
Gets them to treat with him in privacy,
But violates his honour, and his word,
And Villaine-like, there puts them to the sword.
The *Greeks*, having their valiant Captaines slaine,
Chose *Xenophon*, to lead them home again;
But *Tyssaphern* did what he could devise,
To stop the way in this their enterprise,
But when through difficulties still they brake,
He sought all sustinance from them to take,
Before them burnt the country as they went,
So to 'eprive them of all nourishment,
But on they march, through hunger, and through cold,
O're mountains, rocks, and hils, as Lions bold,

No

Nor rivers course, nor *Persians* force could stay,
But on to *Trabezond* they kept their way;
There was of *Greeks*, setled a Colony,
These after all, receiv'd them joyfully:
There for some time they were, but whilst they staid,
Into *Bubynia* often inrodes made,
The King afraid what further they might doe,
Unto the *Spartan* Admirall did sue,
Straight to transport them to the other side,
For these incursions he durst not abide;
So after all their travell, danger, pain,
In peace they saw their Native soyl again
The *Greeks* now (as the *Persian* King suspects)
The *Afiatiques*, cowardize detects,
The many victories themselves did gain,
The many thousand *Persians* they had slain,
And now their Nation with facility,
Might win the universall Monarchy,
They then *Dercillidis*, send with an Hoast,
Who with his *Spartans* on the *Asian* coast,
Town after town, with small resistance take,
Which rumor makes great *Artaxerxes* quake;
The *Greeks* by this successe, incourag'd so,
Agesilaus himself doth over goe,
By th' Kings Lieutenant is encountered,
But *Tyssaphernes* with his Army fled,
Which over-throw incens'd the King so sore,
That *Tyssapherne* must be Vice-roy no more,
Tythraustes now is placed in his stead,
And hath command, to take the others head,
Of that false perjur'd wretck, this was the last,
Who of his cruelty made many tast,

Tythraustes

Tythraustes trusts more to his wit then Arms,
And hopes by craft to quit his Masters harmes,
He knows that many towns in *Greece* envies
The *Spartans* height, which now apace doth rise,
To these he thirty thousand *Tallents* sent,
With suit, their force, against his foes be bent;
They to their discontent, receiving hire,
With broyls, and quarrels, sets all *Greece* on fire.
Agesilaus is called home with speed,
To defend, more then offend, he had need.
They now lost all, and were a peace to make,
The Kings conditions they are forc't to take;
Dissention in *Greece* continued long,
Til many a Captain fel, both wise, and strong,
Whose courage nought but death could ever tame
'Mongst these *Epaminondas* wants no fame,
Who had (as noble *Raleigh* doth evince)
All the peculiar vertues of a Prince.
But let us leave these *Greeks*, to discord bent,
And turne to *Persia*, as is pertinent,
The King from forraign foes, and all at ease,
His home-bred troub'es seeketh to appease,
The two Queens, by his means, 'gin to abate
Their former envie, and inveterate hate,
Then in voluptuousnesse he leads his life,
And weds his Daughter for a second wife,
His Mothers wicked counsell was the cause,
Who sooths him up, his owne desires are Lawes;
But yet for all his greatnesse, and long reign,
He must leave all, and in the pit remain;
Forty three years he rules, then turns to dust,
As all the mighty ones, have done, and must.

Bu.

But this of him is worth the memory,
He was the Master of good *Nehemie.*

Darius Ochus.

GReat *Artaxerxes* dead, *Ochus* succeeds,
Of whom no Record s extant of his deeds;
Was it because the *Grecians* now at war,
Made Writers work at home, they sought not far?
Or dealing with the *Persian,* now no more
Their Acts recorded not, as heretofore?
Or else, perhaps the deeds of *Persian* Kings
In after wars were burnt, 'mongst other things?
That three and twenty years he reign'd, I finde,
The rest is but conjecture of my minde.

Arsames, or Arses.

WHy *Arsames* his brother should succeed,
I can no reason give, cause none I read;
It may be thought, surely he had no Son,
So fell to him, which else it had not done.
What Acts he did, time hath not now left pend,
But as 'tis thought, in him had *Cyrus* end.
Whose race long time had worn the Diadem,
But now's divolved, to another Stem.
Three years he reign'd, as Chronicles expresse,
Then Natures debt he paid, quite Issue-lesse.

Darius

Darius Codomanus.

HOw this *Darius* did attain the Crown,
By favour, force, or fraud, is not set down:
If not (as is before) of *Cyrus* race,
By one of these, he must obtain the place.
Some writers say, that he was *Arses* son,
And that great *Cyrus* line, yet was not run,
That *Ochus* unto *Arsames* was father,
Which by some probabilities (seems rather,)
That son, and father, both were murthered
By one *Bagoas*, an Eunuch (as is sed)
Thus learned *Pemble*, whom we may not slight,
But as before doth (well read) *Raleigh* write,
Antd he that story reads, shall often find,
That severall men, will have their severall mind,
Yet in these differences, we may behold,
With our judicious learned Knight to hold
And this 'mongst all's no controverted thing,
That this *Darius* was last *Per an* King,
Whose warres and losses we may better tell;
In *Alexanders* reign who did him quell,
How from the top of worlds felicity,
He fell to depth of greatest misery,
Whose honours, treasures, pleasures, had short stay;
One deluge came, and swept them all away,
And in the sixt year of his hiplesse reigne,
Of all, did scarce his winding sheet retaine
And last, a sad catastrophe to end,
Him, to the grave, did Traytor *Bessus* send.

The end of the Persian Monarchy.

The third Monarchy was
the *Grecian*, beginning un-
der *Alexander* the Great, in
the 112 *Olimpiad*.

Reat *Alexander*, was wise *Phillips* son,
He, to *Amintas*, Kings of *Macedon*,
The cruell, proud, *Olimpias*, was his mo-
ther,
Shee to the rich *Molossus* King, was
daughter

This Prince (his father by *Pausanias* slain)
The twenty first of's age, began to reign
Great were the gifts of nature, which he had,
His Education, such to these did adde
By Art, and Nature both, he was made fit,
T'accomplish that, which long before was writ
The very day of his activity,
Ioth ground was burnt, *Diana's* Temple high,
An Omen to their near approaching woe,
Whose glory to the Earth, this Prince did throw,
His rule to Greece, he scorn'd should be confin'd
The universe, scarce bounds his large vast minde,

Th

This is the hee goat, which from *Greece* came,
Who ran in fury, on the *Persian* Ram,
That broke his hornes, that threw him on the ground,
To save him from his might, no man was found
Phillip, on this great conquest had an eye,
But death did terminate those thoughts so nigh
The *Greeks* had chose him Captain Generall,
Which honour to his son, now did befall
(For as worlds Monarch, now we speak not o't,
Put as the King of little *Macedon*)
Restlesse both day and night, his heart now was
His high resolves which way to bring to passe
Yet for a while, in *Greece* is forc'd to stay,
Which makes each moment seem, more then a day
Thebs, and old *Athens*, both 'gainst him rebell,
But he their mutinies, full soon doth quell
This done, against all right, and natures Laws,
His kinsmen puts to death without least cause,
That no combustion in his absence be,
In seeking after Sovereignty
And many more, whom he suspects will clambe,
Now taste of death, (least they deserve it more)
Not wonder is't, if he in blood begin,
For cruelty, was his parentall sin
Thus afed now, of troubles and of fears,
His course to *Asia*, next Spring he steers
Leaves sage *Antipater*, at home to sway
And through the *Hellespont*, his ships make way
Comming to land, his dart on shore he throwes,
Then with alacrity he after goes
Thirty two thousand made up his foot force,
To these were joyn'd, five thousand goodly horse

Then on he march'd, in's way he vew'd old *Troy*,
And on *Achilles* Tombe, with wondrous joy,
He offer'd, and for good successe did pray
To him, his mothers Ancestor (men say)
When newes of *Alexander*, came to th' Court,
To scorn at him, *Darius* had good sport:
Sends him a frothy, and contemptuous letter,
Stiles him disloyall servant, and no better,
Reproves him, for his proud audacity,
To lift his hand, 'gainst such a Monarchy.
Then to his Lieutenant, in *Asia* sends,
That he be tane alive, (for he intends)
To whip him well with rods, and then to bring,
That boy so mallepart, before the king
Ah ' fond vaine man, whose pen was taught ere while,
In lower termes to write a higher stile,
To th' river *Granicke*, *Alexander* hyes,
Which twixt *Phrigia*, and *Propontis* lyes.
The *Persians* for encounter ready stand,
And think to keep his men from off the land,
Those banks so steep, the *Greeks*, now scramble up
And beat the coward *Persians* from the top,
And twenty thousand, of their lives bereave,
Who in their backs did all their wounds receive
This Victory did *Alexander* gain,
With losse of thirty four, of his there slaine:
Sardu, then he, and *Ephesus*, did gaine,
Where stood of late *Diana's*, wondrous Phane,
And by *Parmenio* (of renowned fame)
Miletus, and *Pamphylia* overcame,
Halicarnassus and *Pisidia*
He for his master takes, with *Lycia*

Next

Next *Alexander* marcht, t'wards the black sea ,
And easily takes old *Gorduum* in his way ,
(Or Asse-eard)*Midas*, once the regall seat,
Whose touch turn'd all to gold,yea even his meat:
There the Prophetick knot, he cuts in twain;
Which who so did, must Lord of all remain,
Now newes, of *Memnons* death (the Kings Vice-roy)
To *Alexanders* heart's no little joy
For in that Peer, more valour did abide,
Then in *Darius* multitudes beside
There *Arsemes* was plac'd ,yet durst not stay,
But s rs one in his roome, and ran away
His substitute, as fearfull as his master,
Goes after too,and leaves all to disaster.
Now *Alexander* all *Cilicia* takes.
No stroake for it he struck, their hearts so quakes.
To *Greece* he thirty thousand talents sends ,
To raise more force, for what he yet intends.
And on he goes *Darius* so to meet,
Who came with thousand thousands at his feet,
Though some there be, and that more likely,write,
He but four hundred thousand had to fight,
The rest attendants, which made up no lesse;
(Both sexes there) was almost numberlesse.
For this wise King had brought to see the sport,
Along with him, the Ladyes of the Court.
His mother old,beautious wife,and daughters,
It seemes to see the *Macedonians* slaughters.
Sure its beyond my time, and little Art,
To shew,how great *Darius* plaid his part
The splendor, and the pompe, he marched in,
For since the world,was no such Pageant seen

Oh 'twas a goodly fight, there to behold,
The *Persians* clad in filk, and glitt'ring gold,
The ftately Horfes tript, the launces guilt,
As if they were, now all to fun at tilt:
The Holy fire, was borne before the Hoft
(For Sun and Fire the *Perfians* worfhip moft)
The Priefts in their ftrange habit follow after;
An object not fo much of fen, as laughter
The King fat in a chariot made of gold,
With Robes and Crowne, moft glorious to behold.
And o're his head, his golden gods on high,
Support a party coloured canopy
A number of fpare horfes next were led,
Leaft he fhould need them, in his chariots ftead.
But they that faw him in this ftate to lye,
Would think he neither thought to fight nor fly,
He fifteen hundred had like women dreft,
For fo to fright the *Greeks* he judg'd was beft,
Their golden Ornaments fo to fet forth,
Would afke more time, then were their bodys worth.
Great *Sifigambis*, fhe brought up the Reare,
Then fuch a world of Wagons did appear,
Like feverall houfes moving upon wheeles
As if fhe'd drawne, whole *Suffan* at her heeles.
This brave Virago, to the King was mother,
And is much good fhe did, as any other.
Now leaft this Gold, and all this goodly ftuffe,
Had not been fpoile, and booty rich enough,
A thoufand Mules, and Camells ready wait.
Loaden with gold, with Jewels and with Plate,
For fure *Darius* thought at the firft fight,
The *Greeks* would all adore, and would none fight.

But

But when both Armies met, he might behold,
That valour was more worth then Pearls, or gold,
And how his wealth serv'd but for baits t'allure,
Which made his over throw more fierce, and sure.
The *Greeks* come on, and with a gallant grace,
Let fly their Arrowes, in the *Persians* face,
The cowards feeling this sharp stinging charge,
Most basely run, and left their King at large,
Who from his golden Coach is glad t'alight,
And cast away his Crown, for swifter flight;
Of late like some immovable he lay,
Now finds both leggs, and Horse, to run away,
Two hundred thousand men that day were slaine,
And forty thousand Prisoners also tane,
Besides, the Queens, and Lad es of the Court,
If *Curtius* be true, in his report.
The Regall ornaments now lost, the treasure
Divided at the *Macedonians* pleasure.
Yet all this grief, this losse, this over-throw,
Was but beginning of his future woe,
The Royall Captives, brought to *Alexander*,
T'ward them, demean'd himself like a Commander,
For though their beauties were unparalled
Conquer'd himself (now he had conquered)
Preserv'd their honour, us'd them courteously,
Commands, no man should doe them injury,
And this to *Alexander* is more a fame,
Then that the *Persian* King he over-came,
Two hundred eighty *Greeks* he lost in fight,
By too much heat, not wounds (as Authors write)
No sooner had this Captain won the field,
But all *Phenicia* to his pleasures yeeld,

Of

Of which, the Government he doth commit
Unto *Parmenio*, of all, most fit ,
Darius now, more humble then before,
Writes unto *Alexander*, to restore
Those mournfull Ladies, from captivity,
For whom he offers him a ransome high ,
But down his haughty stomach could not bring,
To give this Conquerour, the stile of King ,
His Letter *Alexander* doth disdaine,
And in short termes, sends this reply againe :
A King he was, and that not only so,
But of *Darius* King, as he should know.
Now *Alexander* unto *Tyre* doth goe,
(His valour, and his victories they know)
To gain his love, the *Tyrians* do intend,
Therefore a Crown, and great provisions send ,
Their present he receives with thankfulnesse,
Desires to offer unto *Hercules*,
Protector of their Town , by whom defended,
And from whom also, lineally descended :
But they accept not this, in any wise,
Least he intend more fraud, then sacrifice ,
Sent word, that *Hercules* his Temple stood,
In the old town (which now lay like a wood)
With this reply, he was so sore enrag'd,
To win their town, his honour he engag'd ;
And now, as *Babels* King did once before,
He leaves not, till he makes the sea firme shoar,
But far lesse cost, and time, he doth expend,
The former ruines, help to him now lend ;
Besides, he had a Navie at command,
The other by his men fetcht all by Land ,

In

In seven months space he takes this lofty town,
Whose glory, now a second time's brought down ;
Two thousand of the cheif he crucifi'd,
Eight thousand by the sword now also dy'd,
And thirteen thousand Gally slaves he made,
And thus the *Tyrians* for mistrust were paid,
The rule of this he to *Philotas* give,
Who was the Son of that *Parmenio* brave ,
Cilicia he to *Socrates* doth give,
For now's the time, Captains like Kings may live ;
For that which easily comes, as freely goes ,
Zidon he on *Ephestion* bestowes .
He scorns to have one worse then had the other,
And therefore gives this Lord ship to another.
Ephestion now, hath the command o' th' Fleet,
And must at *Gaza*, *Alexander* meet ;
Darius finding troubles still increase,
By his Embassadours now sues for peace.
And layes before great *Alexanders* eyes,
The dangers, difficulties, like to rise ,
First, at *Euphrates*, what he's like to abide,
And then at *Tigris*, and *Araxes* side .
These he may scape, and if he so desire,
A league of friendship make firm, and entire ,
His eldest Daughter, (him) in marriage offers,
And a most Princely Dowry with her proffers,
All those rich Kingdoms large, which doe abide
Betwixt the H*ellespont*, and *Halhs* side ,
But he with scorn, his courtesie rejects,
And the distressed King no way respects,
Tels him, these proffers great (in truth were none)
For all he offered now, was but his owne :

But

But, quoth *Parmenio*, (that brave Commander)
Was I as great, as is great *Alexander*,
Darius offers I would not reject,
But th' Kingdoms, and the Ladies, soone accept ;
To which, brave *Alexander* did reply,
And so if I *Parmenio* were, would I
He now to *Gaza* goes, and there doth meet
His favourite *Epheftion*, with his fleet ,
Where valiant *Betis*, doth defend the town,
(A loyall Subject to *Darius* Crown)
For more repulse, the *Grecians* here abide,
Then in the *Persian* Monarchy Leside ,
And by these walls, so many men were slaine,
That *Greece* must yeeld a fresh supply againe ,
But yet, this well defended town is taken,
(For 'twas decreed, that Empire should be shaken)
The Captaine tane, had holes bor'd through his feet,
And by command was drawn through every street,
To imitate *Achilles* (in his shame)
Who did the like to *Hector* (of more fame)
What, hast thou lost thy late magnanimity?
Can *Alexander* deale thus cruelly ?
Sith valour, with Hereyicks is renown'd,
Though in an enemy it should be found ,
If of thy future fame thou hadst regard,
Why didst not heap up honour, and reward ?
From *Gaza*, to *Jerusalem* he goes,
But in no hostile way (as I suppose)
Him in his Priestly Robes, high *Jaddus* meets,
Whom with great reverence *Alexander* greets ;
The Priest shews him good *Daniels* Prophesie,
How he should over throw this Monarchy ,

By

By which he was so much incouraged,
No future dangers he did ever dread.
From thence, to fruitfull Ægypt marcht with speed,
Where happily in's wars he did succeed.
To see how fast he gain'd, is no small wonder,
For in few dives he brought that Kingdom under.
Then to the house of Jupiter, he went,
For to be call'd a god, was his intent;
The Pagan Priest through hire, or else mistake,
The Son of Jupiter did straight him make:
He Diabolicall must needs remaine,
That his humanity will not retaine;
Now back to Ægypt goes, and in few dayes,
Faire Alexandria from the ground doth raise,
Then setling all things in lesse Asia,
In Syria, Ægypt and Phœnicia:
Unto Euphrates marcht, and over goes,
For no man to resist his valour showes,
Had Betis now been there, but with his Band,
Great Alexander had been kept from Land;
But as the King is, so's the multitude,
And now of valour both were destitute;
Yet he (poore Prince) another Hoast doth muster,
Of Persians, Scithians, Indians, in a cluster;
Men but in shape, and name, of valour none,
Fit for to blunt the swords of Macedon;
Two hundred fifty thousand by account,
Of Horse, and Foot, this Army did amount;
For in his multitudes his trust still lay,
But on their fortitude he had small stay;
Yet had some hope, that on that eeven plain,
His numbers might the victory obtaine.

About

About this time, *Darius* beauteous Queen,
Who had long travaile, and much sorrow seen,
Now bids the world adieu, her time being spent,
And leaves her wofull Lord for to lament.
Great *Alexander* mourns, as well as he,
For this lost Queen (though in captivity)
When this sad newes (at first) *Darius* heares,
Some injury was offered, he feares,
But when inform'd, how royally the King
Had used her, and hers, in every thing,
He prayes the immortall gods, for to reward
Great *Alexander*, for this good regard ;
And if they down, his Monarchy wil throw,
Let them on him, that dignity bestow :
And now for peace he sues, as once before,
And offers all he did, and Kingdoms more,
His eldest Daughter, for his Princely Bride,
(Nor was such match, in all the world beside)
And all those Countries, which (betwixt) did lye,
Phenisian Sea, and great *Euphrates* high,
With fertile *Ægypt*, and rich *Syria*,
And all those Kingdoms in lesse *Asia* ;
With thirty thousand Tallents, to be paid
For his Queen-Mother, and the royall Maid,
And till all this be wel perform'd, and sure,
Ochus his Son a hostage shall endure
To this, stout *Alexander*, gives no eare,
No, though *Parmenio* plead, he will not heare ;
Which had he done (perhaps) his fame had kept,
Nor infamy had wak'd, when he had slept,
For his unlimited prosperity,
Him boundlesse made, in vice, and cruelty ,

K   Thus

Thus to *Darius* he writes back again,
The Firmament two Suns cannot contain;
Two Monarchies on Earth cannot abide,
Nor yet two Monarchs in one World reside,
The afflicted King, finding him set to jar,
Prepares against to morrow for the war,
Parmenio, Alexander wisht, that night,
To force his Camp, so put them all to flight,
For tumult in the dark doth cause most dread,
And weaknesse of a foe is covered,
But he disdain'd to steale a victorie,
The Sun should witnesse of his valour be:
Both Armies meet, *Greeks* fight, the *Persians* run,
So make an end, before they well begun,
Forty five thousand *Alexander* had,
But 'tis not known what slaughters here they made.
Some write, th' other had a million, some more,
But *Quintus Curtius*, as was said before.
At *Arbela*, this victory was gain'd,
And now with it, the town also obtain'd.
Darius stript of all, to *Media* came,
Accompani'd with sorrow, fear, and shame,
At *Arbela* left, his ornaments, and treasure,
Which *Alexander* deals, as suits his pleasure
This Conquerour now goes to *Babylon*,
Is entertain'd with joy, and pompous train,
With showres of Flowers, the streets along are strown,
And Insence burnt, the silver Altars on,
The glory of the Castle he admires,
The firme foundations, and the lofty spires;
In this a masse of gold, and treasure lay,
Which in few hours was carried all away,

With

With greedy eyes, he views this City round,
Whose fame throughout the world, was so renown'd ;
And to possesse, he counts no little blisse,
The Towers, and Bowers, of proud *Semiramis* :
Though worn by time, and raz'd by foes full fore,
Yet old foundations shew'd, and somewhat more ;
With all the pleasures that on earth was found,
This City did abundently abound ,
Where four and thirty dayes he now doth stay,
And gives himself to banqueting, and play :
He, and his Souldiers, wax effeminate,
And former Discipline begins to hate ;
Whilst revelling at *Babylon,* he lyes,
Antipater, from *Greece,* sends great supplyes,
He then to *Sushan* goes, with his fresh bands,
But needs no force, 'tis rend'red to his hands ;
He likewise here a world of treasure found,
For 'twas the seat of *Persian* Kings renown'd ;
Here stood the Royall houses of delight,
Where Kings have shown their glory, wealth, and might;
The sumptuous Palace of Queen *Hester* here,
And of good *Mordecai,* her Kin'man dear ;
Those purp'e hangings, mixt with green, and white,
Those beds of gold, and couches of delight,
And furniture, the richest of all Lands,
Now falls into the *Macedonians* hands.
From *Sushan,* to *Persepolis* he goes,
Which newes doth still augment *Darius* woes,
In his approach, the Governour sends word,
For his receit with joy, they'l accord,
With open Gates, the wealthy town did stand,
And all in it was at his high command ,

Of all the Cities, that on Earth was found,
None like to this in riches did abound
Though *Babylon* was rich, and *Sushan* too,
Yet to compare with this, they might not do.
Here lay the bulk, of all those precious things,
Which did pertain unto the *Persian* Kings.
For when the Souldiers, had rifled their pleasure,
And taken mony, plate, and golden treasure,
Statues of gold, and silver numberlesse,
Yet after all, as stories do expresse.
The share of *Alexander* did amount,
To a hundred thousand Tallents by account.
Here of his own, he sets a Garrison,
(As first at *Sushan*, and at *Babylon*)
On their old Governours, titles he laid,
But on their faithfullnesse, he never staid.
Their charge, gave to his Captains (as most just)
For such revolters false, what Prince will trust.
The pleasures and the riches of this town,
Now makes this King, his vertues all to drown
He walloweth now, in all licenciousnesse,
In pride, and cruelty, to th' highest excesse.
Being inflam'd with wine upon a season,
(Fil'ed with madnesse, and quite void of reason)
He at a bold, base Strumpets, lewd desire;
Commands to set this goodly town on fire.
Parke no wise, intreats him to desist,
And layes before his eyes, if he persist
His names dishonour, losse unto his State.
And just procuring of the *Persians* hate
But deafe to reason, (bent to have his will,)
Those stately streets with raging flames doth fil.

Now

Now to *Darius*, he directs his way,
Who was retir'd, and gone to *Media.*
(And there with sorrows, fears, and cares surrounded)
Had now his fourth, and last Army compounded,
Which forty thousand made, but his intent,
Was straight in *Bactria* these to augment,
But hearing, *Alexander* was so near,
Thought now this once, to try his fortunes here,
Chusing rather an honorable death·
Then still with infamy, to draw his breath.
But *Bessus* false, who was his cheife Commander;
Perswades him not to fight, with *Alexander*
With sage advice, he layes before his eyes,
The little hope, of profit like to rise.
If when h'd multitudes, the day he lost,
Then with so few, how likely to be crost.
This counsell, for his safety, he pretended,
But to deliver him to's foes, intended.
Next day this treason, to *Darius* known,
Transported sore, with griefe and passion;
Grinding his teeth, and plucking off his haire,
down o're whelm'd, with sorrow, and despair,
Bidding his servant *Artabasus* true,
Look to himselfe, and leave him to that crew,
Who was of hopes, and comfort quite bereft,
And of his Guard, and Servrets now left
Straight *Bessus* comes, and with his traiterous hands,
Layes hold on's Lord, and binding him with bands
Into a cart him throwes, covered with hides,
Who wanting means t resist these wrongs abides
Then draws the Cart along, with chaines of gold,
In more despight, the thralled Prince to hold

And

And thus to *Alexander*, on he goes,
Great recompence, in's thoughts, he did propose,
But some detesting, this his wicked fact,
To *Alexander* fly, and told this act,
Who doubling of his march, posts in amain,
Darius from those Traitors him to gain,
Bessus gets knowledge, his disloyalty,
Hid *Alexanders* wrath incensed high,
Whose Army now, was almost within sight,
His hopes being dasht, prepares himself for flight.
Unto *Darius*, first he brings a Horse,
And bids him, save himself, by speedy course.
This wofull King, his courtesie refuses,
Whom thus the execrable wretch abuses
By throwing Darts, gives him his mortall wound,
Then slew his servants, that were faithfull found,
Yea, wounds the beasts (that drew him) unto death,
And leaves him thus to gaspe out his last breath.
(*Bessus*, his Partner in this Tragedy,
Was the false Governour of *Bactria*.)
This done, they with their Horse, soon speed away,
To hide themselves, remote in *Bactria*,
Disturb'd in's thoughts, sends out his greatnes,
Invokes the Heavens, and earth, to mourn his moanes,
His lost felicity did grieve him sore,
But this unheard of injury much more,
Yea, above all, that in such case, never was.
Should here, now fear, his crowns, and misery,
As thus he lay, *Polystratus* a *Greeke*,
Wearied with his long march, did water seek,
So chanc'd these bloody Horses to espy,
Whose wounds had made their skins of purple dye,

T̕

To them he goes, and looking in the Cart,
Findes poore *Darius*, peirced to the heart,
Who not a little chear'd, to have some eye,
The witnesse of his dying misery
Prayes him, to *Alexander* to commend,
The just revenge of this his wofull end,
And not to pardon such disloyalty,
Of treason, murther, and base cruelty.
If not, because *Darius* thus did pray,
Yet that succeeding Kings in safety may
Their lives enjoy, their crowns, and dignity,
And not by Traitors hands untimely dye
He also sends his humble thankfulnesse,
For all that Kingly Grace he did expresse,
To's Mother, Children deare, and Wife now one,
Which made their long restraint, seeme to be none,
Praying the immortall gods, that Sea, and Land
Might be subiected to his royall hand.
And that his rule as farre extended be,
As men, the rising, setting Sun shall see
This said, the *Greek* for water doth intreat,
To quench his thirst, and to allay his heat,
Of all good things (quoth he) once in my power,
I've nothing left, at th's my dying houre,
Thy pitty, and compassion to reward,
Wherefore the gods require thy made regard.
This said, his fainting breath did steer away,
And though a Monarch once, now lyes like clay,
Yea, thus must every Son of *Adam* lye,
Though gods on earth, like Sons of men shall dye.
Now to the East great *Alexander* goes,
To see if any durst his might oppose,

K   (For

(For scarce the world, or any bounds thereon,
Could bound his boundlesse, fond ambition)
Such as submits, he doth againe restore,
And makes their riches, and their honours more ;
On *Artabasus* more then all bestow'd,
For his fidelity to 's Master show'd ,
Thalestris, Queen of th' *Amazons*, now brought
Her traine to *Alexander* (as 'tis thought)
Though some of reading best, and sound st minde,
Such country there, nor yet such people finde.
Then tell her errand, we had better spare
To th' ignorant, her title may declare
As *Alexander* in his greatnesse growes,
So daily of his vertues doth he lose ;
He basenesse counts his former clemency,
And not beseeming such a dignity ,
His past sobriety doth also hate,
As most incompatible to his state ;
His temperance, is but a sordid thing,
No wayes becomming such a mighty King ,
His greatnesse now he takes, to represent,
His fancied gods, above the firmament,
And such as shew'd but reverence before,
Are strictly now commanded to adore ;
With *Persian* Robes, himselfe doth dignifie,
Charging the same on his Nobility ;
His manners, habit, gestures, now doth fashion,
After that conquer'd, and luxurious Nation ,
His Captains, that were vertuously enclin'd,
Griev'd at this change of manners, and of minde ;
The ruder sort, did openly deride
His famed Deity, and foolish pride ;

The

The certainty of both comes to his eares,
But yet no notice takes, of what he hears;
With thofe of worth, he ftill defires efteem,
So heaps up gifts, his credit to redeem;
And for the reft new wars, and travels findes,
That other matters may take up their minds.
Then hearing, *Beffus* makes himfelfe a King,
Intends with fpeed, that Traitor down to bring;
Now that his Hoaft from luggage might be free,
And no man with his burden, burdened be,
Commands forth-with, each man his fardle bring,
Into the Market place, before the King.
Which done, fets fire upon thofe coftly fpoyls
The recompence of travels, wars, and toyls,
And thus unwifely, in one raging fume,
The wealth of many Cities doth confume:
But marvell 'tis, that without muteny,
The Souldiers fhould let paffe this injury;
Nor wonder leffe, to Readers may it bring,
For to obferve the rafhneffe of the King.
Now with his Army, doth he haft away,
Falfe *Beffus* to finde out, in *Bactria*,
But fore diftreft for water, in their march,
The drought, and heat, their bodies much doth parch;
At length, they came to th' River *Oxus* brink,
Where moft immoderatly thefe thirfty drink;
This more mortality to them did bring,
Then did their wars, againft the *Perfian* King.
Here *Alexander*'s almoft at a ftand,
How to paffe over, and gaine the other Land;
For Boats here's none, nor neare it any wood,
To make them rafts, to waft them o're the floud;

But

But he that was resolved in his minde,
Would by some means a transportation finde;
So from his carriages the Hides he takes,
And stuffing them with straw, he bundles makes,
On these, together ty'd, in six dayes space,
They all passe over, to the other place,
Hid *Bessus* had but valour to his wil,
He easily might have made them stay there stil :
But coward, durst not fight, nor could he fly,
Hated of all, for's former treachery,
Is by his owne, now bound in Iron chaines,
(A coller of the same his neck containes)
And in this sort, they rather drag, then bring,
This Malefactor vild, before the King,
Who to *Darius* Brother gives the wretch,
With wracks, and tortures, every limbe to stretch,
Here was of *Greeks*, a town in *Bactria*,
Whom *Xerxes* from their country led away ;
These not a little joy'd, this day to see,
Wherein their own had soveraignity.
And now reviv'd with hopes, held up their head,
From bondage, long to be infranchised ,
But *Alexander* puts them to the sword,
Without cause, given by them, in deed, or word :
Nor sex, nor age, nor one, nor other spar'd,
But in his cruelty alike they shar'd ,
Nor could he reason give, for this great wrong,
But that they had forgot their Mother-tongue.
Whilst thus he spent some time in *Bactria*,
And in his Camp strong, and securely lay,
Down from the mountains twenty thousand came,
And there most fiercely set upon the same ,

Repelling

Repelling thefe two marks of honour got,
Imprinted deep in's legg, by Arrowes fhot,
And now the *Bactrus* 'gainft him rebel,
But he their ftubbornneffe full foone doth quel;
From hence he to *Taxartis* river goes,
Where *Scithians* rude, his valour doen oppofe,
And with their out cries, in a hideous fort,
Befets his Camp, or Military Court;
Of Darts, and Arrowes, made fo little fpare,
They flew fo thicke they feem'd to dark the aire:
But foone the *Grecians* forc'd them to a flight,
Whofe nakedneffe could not endure their might,
Upon this Rivers banck in feventeen dayes,
A goodly City doth compleatly raife,
Which *Alexandria* he doth alfo name,
And furlongs fixty could not round the fame.
His third fupply, *Antipater* now fent,
Which did his former Army much augment,
And being an hundred twenty thoufand ftrong,
He enters now the *Indian* Kings among;
Thofe that fubmit, he doth reftore again.
Thofe that doe not, both they, and theirs, are flain;
To age, nor fex, no pitty doth expreffe,
But all fall by his fword, moft merciteffe,
He t' *Nifa* goes, by *Bacchus* built long fince,
Whofe feafts are celebrated by this Prince,
Nor had that drunken god, one that would take
His liquors more devoutly in, for's fake.
When thus, ten dayes, his brain with wine he'd foak'd,
And with delicious meats, his Pallat choak'd,
To th' river *Indus* next, his courfe he bends,
Boats to prepare, *Epheftion* firft he fends,

Who,

Who comming thither, long before his Lord;
Hid to his mind, made all things now accord :
The Veſſells ready were, at his command ;
And *Omphis*, King of that part of the land:
Through his perſwaſion *Alexander* meets;
And as his Sovereign Lord him humbly greets.
Fifty ſix Elephants he brings to's hands:
And tenders him the ſtrength of all his lands,
Preſents himſelſe, there with a golden Crowne,
And eighty Tallents to his Captaines down.
But *Alexander*, caus'd him to behold,
He glory ſought, no ſilver, nor yet gold ;
His Preſents all, with thanks he doth reſtore,
And of his own, a thouſand Tallents more.
Thus all the *Indian* Kings, to him ſubmit ,
But *Porus* ſtout, who will not yeeld as yet ,
To him doth *Alexander* thus declare,
His pleaſure is, that forthwith he repaire
Unto his Kingdoms borders, and as due,
His Homage unto him as Soveraigne doe.
But Kingly *Porus* this brave anſwer ſent,
That to attend him there, was his intent ;
And come as well provided as he could,
But for the reſt, his ſword adviſe him ſhould
Great *Alexander* vext at this reply,
Did more his valour then his Crown envie ;
Is now reſolv'd to paſſe *Hidaſpes* floud,
And there his Soveraignty for to make good ;
But on the banks doth *Porus* ready ſtand,
For to receive him, when he comes to land ,
A potent Army with him, like a King,
And ninety Elephants for war did bring ,

Had

Had *Alexander* such resistance seen,
On *Tygris* side, here now he had not been,
Within this spacious river, deep, and wide,
Did here, and there, Isles full of trees abide;
His Army *Alexander* doth divide,
With *Ptolomy*, sends part o' th' tother side.
Porus encounters them, thinking all's there,
Then covertly, the rest gets o're else where,
But whilst the first he valiantly assayl'd,
The last set on his back, and so prevail'd:)
Yet work enough, here *Alexander* found,
For to the last, stout *Porus* kept his ground.
Nor was't dishonour, at the length to yeeld,
When *Alexander* strives to win the field,
His fortitude his Kingly foe commends;
Restores him, and his bounds further extends,
East-ward, now *Alexander* would goe still,
But so to doe, his Souldiers had no will,
Long with excessive travailes wearied,
Could by no meaus be further drawn, or led:
Yet that his fame might to posterity,
Be had in everlasting memory,
Doth for his Camp a greater circuit take,
And for his Souldiers larger Cabins make,
His Maungers he erected up so high,
As never Horse his Provender could eye,
Huge Bridles made, which here, and there, he left,
Which might be found, and so for wonders kept.
Twelve Altars, he for Monuments then rears,
Whereon his acts, and travels, long appears;
But doubting, wearing Time would these decay,
And so his memory might fade away,

He

He on the faire *Hidaspis* pleasant side,
Two Cities built, his fame might there abide;
The first *Nicea*, the next *Bucephalon*,
Where he entomb'd his stately Stallion.
His fourth, and last supply, was hither sent,
Then down t' *Hidaspis* with his Fleet he went;
Some time he after spent upon that shore,
Where one hundred Embassadours, or more,
Came with submission, from the *Indian* Kings
Bringing their Presents rare, and precious things:
These, all he feasts in state, on beds of gold,
His furniture most sumptuous to behold;
The meat, and drink, attendants, every thing,
To th' utmost shew'd, the glory of a King;
With rich rewards, he sent them home again,
Acknowledg'd for their Masters Soveraigne;
Then sayling South and comming to the shore,
These obscure Nations yeelded as before,
A City here he built, cal'd by his name,
Which could not sound or oft, with too much fame,
Hence sayling down by th' mouth of *Indus* floud,
His Gallies stuck upon the sand, and mud;
Which the stout *Oxedonians* maz'd sore
Depriv'd at once, the use of saile, and Oare,
But well observing th' nature of the tide,
Upon those Flats they did not long abide;
Passing faire *Indus* mouth, his course he stear'd,
To th' coast which by *Euphrates* mouth appear'd,
Whose inlets neare unto, he winter spent,
Unto his starved Souldiers small content,
By hunger, and by cold, so many shine,
That of them all, the fourth did scarce remaine.

                        Thus

Thus Winter, Souldiers, and provision spent,
From hence he to *Gedrosia* went,
And thence he marcht into *Carmania*,
So he at length drew neare to *Persia*,
Now through these goodly countries as he past,
Much time in feasts, and ryoting doth wast,
Then visits *Cyrus* Sepulcher in's way,
Who now obscure at *Passagardis* lay,
Upon his Monument his Robes he spread,
And set his Crown on his supposed head,
From hence to *Babylon*, some time there spent,
He at the last to royall *Sushan* went,
A Wedding Feast to's Nobles then he makes,
And *Statira*, *Darius* daughter takes,
Her Sister gives to his *Ephestion* deare,
That by this match he might be yet more neare.
He fourscore *Persian* Ladies also gave,
At the same time, unto his Captains brave;
Six thousand Guests he to this feast invites,
Whose Sences all, were glutted with delights:
It far exceeds my meane abilities,
To shadow forth these short felicities:
Spectators here, could scarce relate the story,
They were so wrapt with this externall glory.
If an Ideall Paradise, a man should frame,
He might this feast imagine by the same.
To every Guest, a cup of gold he sends,
So after many dayes this Banquet ends.
Now, *Alexanders* conquests, all are done,
And his long travells past, and over-gone;
His vertues dead, buried, and all forgot,
But vice remaines, to his eternall blot.

'Mongst

'Mongst those, that of his cruelty did taste,
Philotas was not least, nor yet the last ,
Accus'd, because he did not certifie
The King of treason, and conspiracy ;
Upon suspicion being apprehended ,
Nothing was found, wherein he had offended ,
His silence, guilt was, of such consequence,
He death deserv'd, for this so high offence ;
But for his Fathers great deserts, the King,
His Royall pardon gave, for this same thing ;
Yet is *Philotas* unto Judgement brought,
Must suffer, not for what he did, but thought.
His Master is Accuser, Judge, and King,
Who to the height doth aggravate each thing ,
Enveighs against his Father, now absent,
And's Brethren, whom for him their lives had spent ;
But *Philotas*, his unpardonable crime,
Which no merit could obliterate, or time ;
He did the Oracle of *Iupiter* deride,
By which his Majesty was deifi'd.
Philotas thus o're charg'd, with wrong, and greif,
Sunk in despair, without hope of releif ;
Faine would have spoke, and made his owne defence,
The King would give no eare, but went from thence ,
To his malicious foes delivers him,
To wreak their spight, and hate, on every limbe.
Philotas after him sends out this cry,
Oh, *Alexander*, thy free clemency,
My foer exceeds in malice, and their hate,
Thy Kingly word can easily terminate ;
Such torments great, as wit could first invent,
Or flesh, or life could bear, till both were spent

                                              Are

Are now inflicted on *Parmenio's* Son,
For to accuse himself, as they had done,
At last he did   So they were justified,
And told the world, that for desert he dyed.
But how these Captaines should, or yet their Master,
Look on *Parmenio,* after this disaster,
They knew not, wherefore, best now to be done,
Was to dispatch the Father, as the Son.
This sound advice, at heart, pleas'd *Alexander,*
Who was so much engag'd, to this Commander,
As he would ne're confess, nor could reward,
Nor could his Captaines bear so great regard,
Wherefore at once all these to satisfie,
It was decreed *Parmenio* should dye.
Polidamus, who seem'd *Parmenio's* friend,
To doe this deed, they two *Medes* send;
He walking in his Garden, too and fro,
Thinking no harme, because he none did owe,
Most wickedly was slaine, without least crime,
(The most renowned Captaine of his time)
This is *Parmenio,* which so much had done,
For *Philip* dead, and his surviving Son,
Who from a petty King of *Macedon,*
By him was set upon the *Persian* Throne.
This that *Parmenio,* who still over came,
Yet gave his Master the immortall fame;
Who for his prudence, valour, care, and trust,
Had this reward most cruel, and unjust.
The next that in untimely death had put,
Was one of more esteem, but lesse desart,
Clitus, belov'd next to *Ephestion,*
And in his cups, his chief Compinion,

I

Won

When both were drunk, *Clitus* was wont to jeere,
Alexander, to rage, to kill, and sweare,
Nothing more pleasing to mad *Clitus* tongue,
Then's Masters god-head, to defie, and wrong,
Nothing toucht *Alexander* to the quick
Like this, against his deiry to kick :
Upon a time, when both had drunken well,
Upon this dangerous theam fond *Clitus* fell,
From jeast, to earnest, and at last so bold,
That of *Parmenio's* death him plainly told.
Alexander now no longer could containe,
But instantly commands him to be slaine,
Next day, he tore his face, for what he'd done,
And would have slaine himself, for *Clitus* gone,
This pot companion he did more bemoan,
Then all the wrong to brave *Parmenio* done.
The next of worth, that suffered after these,
Was vertuous, learned, wise *Calisthenes*,
Who lov'd his Master more then did the rest,
As did appeare, in flattering him the least .
In his esteem, a God he could not be,
Nor would adore him for a Deity :
For this alone, and for no other cause,
Against his Soveraigne, or against his Lowes,
He on the wrack, his limbs in peeces rent,
Thus was he tortur'd, till his life was spent.
Of this unkingly deed, doth *Seneca*
This censure passe, and not unwisely, say,
Of *Alexander*, this th' eternall crime,
Which shall not be obliterate by time,
Which vertues fame can ne're redeem by fame,
Nor all felicity, of his in war ,

When

When e're 'tis said, he thousand thousands slew,
Yea, and *Calisthines* to death he drew,
The migh y *Persian* King he over-came,
Yea and he kild *Calisthines* by name ,
All Kingdoms, Countries, Provinces, he won,
From *Hellispont*, to th' furthest Ocean ,
All this he did, who knows not to be true,
But yet withall, *Calisthines* he slew ;
From *Macedon* his Empire did extend,
Unto the furthest bounds of th' orient ;
All this he did, yea, and much more, 'tis true,
But yet withall, *Calisthines* he slew.
Now *Alexander* goes to *Media,*
Findes there the want of wise *Parmenio,*
Here his cheif favourite *Ephestion* dyes,
He celebrates his mournfull obsequies ;
For him erects a stately Monument,
Twelve thousand Tallents on .t franckly spent ;
Hangs his Phisitian, the reason why,
Because he let *Ephestion* to dye
This act (me thinks) his god head should ashame,
To punish, where himself deserved blame :
Or of necessity, he must imply,
The other was the greatest Deity
From *Med a* to *Babylon* he went,
To meet him there, t' *Antipater* had sent,
That he might next now act upon the Stage,
And in a Tragedy there end his age
The Queen *Olimpias,* bears him deadly hate,
(Not suffering her to meddle in the State)
And by her Letters did her Son incite,
This great indignity for to require

His doing so, no whit displeas'd the King,
Though to his Mother he disprov'd the thing,
But now, *Antipater* had liv'd thus long,
He might well dye, though he had done no wrong,
His service great now's suddenly forgot,
Or if remembred, yet regarded not,
The King doth intimate 'twas his intent,
His honours, and his riches, to augment
Of larger Provinces, the rule to give,
And for his Counsell, ne're the King to live
So to be caught, *Antipater*'s too wise,
Parmenio's death s too fresh before his eyes,
He was too subtile for his crafty foe,
Nor by his baits could be ensnared so :
But his excuse with humb'e thanks he sends,
His age, and journey long, he now pretends.
And pardon craves, for his unwilling stay,
He shewes his grief, he's forc'd to disobey.
Before his answer came to *Babylon*,
The thread of *Alexanders* life was spun,
Poyson had put an end to's dayes 'twas thought,
By *Philip*, and *Cassander*, to him brought,
Sons to *Antipater*, bearers of his Cup,
Least of such like, their Father chance to sup :
By others thought, and that more generally,
That through excessive drinking he did dye.
The thirty third of's age doe all agree,
This Conquerour did yeeld to destiny,
Whose famous Acts must last, whilst world shall stand,
And Conquests be talkt of, whilst there is Land,
His Princely qualities, had he retain'd
Unparalel'd, for ever had remain'd.

But with the world his vertues overcame,
And so with black, be-clouded all his fame.
Wise *Aristotle*, tutour to his youth,
Had so instructed him in morall truth
The principles of what he then had learn'd
Might to the last (when sober) be discern'd
Learning, and learned men, he much regarded,
And curious Artists evermore rewarded
The Illiads of *Homer* he still kept,
And under's pillow laid them when he slept.
Achilles happinesse he did envy,
'Cause *Homer* kept his Acts to memory ;
Profusely bountifull, without desert,
For those that pleas'd him, had both weal hand heart
Cruell by nature, and by custome too,
As oft his Acts throughout his reigne did shew.
More boundles in ambition then the skie,
Vain thirsting after immortality.
Still fearing that his Name might hap to die,
And fame not last unto Eternity :
This conquerour did oft lament ('tis sed)
There was no world's, more, to be conquered.
This folly great *Augustus* did deride,
For had he had but wisdome to his pride,
He would have found enough for to be done,
To govern that he had already won ·
His thoughts are perish'd he aspires no more,
Nor can he kill, or save as heretofore,
A God alive him all must Idolize,
Now like a mortall helplesse man he lies,
Of all those kingdomes large which he had got,
To his posterity remain'd no jot,

For

For by that hand, which still revengeth bloud,
None of his Kindred, or his Race, long stood,
And as he took delight, much b'oud to spill,
So the same cup to his, did others fill
Four of his Captains, all doe now divide,
As *Daniel*, before had Prophesied,
The Leopard down, his four wings 'gan to rise,
The great Horn broke, the lesse did tyrannize,
What troubles, and contentions did ensue,
We may hereafter shew, in season due.

Aridæus.

GReat *Alexander* dead, his Army's lefe,
Like to that Giant, of his eye bereft,
When of his monstrous bulk it was the guide,
His matchlesse force no Creature could abide,
But by *Ulysses*, having lost his sight,
Each man began for to contemn his might,
For ayming still amisse, his dreadfull blowes
Did harm him self, but never reacht his foes:
New Court, and Camp, all in confusion be,
A King they'l have, but who, none can agree.
Each Captain wisht this prize to beare away,
Yet none io hardy found is so durst say
Great *Alexander* had left issue none,
Except by *Artabazus daughter one;*
And *Roxana* faire, whom late he married,
Was ne're her time to be delivered,
By Natures right, these had enough to claime,
But in earnesse of their Mothers bird the same

Alleadg'd by thofe, which by their fubtill pira
Had hope themfelves, to beare the Crown away,
A Sifter *Alexander* had, but fhe
Claim'd not, perhaps her Sex might hindrance be
After much tumult, they at laft proclaim'd
His bafe born Brother, *Aridæus* nam'd,
That fo under his feeble wit, and reign,
Their en is they might the better ftill attain.
This choyfe *Perdicas*, vehemently difclaim'd,
And th' unborn babe of *Roxan* he proclaim'd;
Some wifhed him, to take the ftile of King,
Becaufe his Mafter gave to him his Ring,
And had to him, ftill fince *Epheftion* dyed,
More then to th' reft, his favour teftified :
But he refus'd, with fained modefty,
Hoping to be eleft more generally ;
He hold of this occafion fhould have laid,
For second offers there were never made ;
'Mongft thefe contentions, tumults, jealoufies,
Seven dayes the Corps of their great Mafter lyes
Untoucht, uncovered, flighted, and neglefted,
So much thefe Princes their owne ends refpefted.
A contemplation to aftonifh Kings,
That he, who late, poffeft all earthly things,
And yet not fo content, unleffe that he
Might be efteemed for a Deity;
Now lay a fpeftacle, to teftifie
The wretchedneffe of mans mortality
After this time, when ftirs began to calme,
The *Egyptians* his body did enbalme,
On which no figne of poyfon could be found,
But all his bowels, cloured well, and found

Perdicas

Perdicas, seeing *Aridæus* must be King,
Under his name begins to rule each thing.
His chief opponents who kept-off the Crown,
Was stiffe *Meleager*, whom he would take down,
Him by a wile he got within his power,
And took his life unworthily that houre :
Using the name, and the command o'th' King
To authorize his Acts in every thing.
The Princes seeing *Perdica's* power and Pride,
Thought timely for themselves now to provide
Antigonus, for his share *Asia* takes,
And *Ptolomy*, next sure of *Egypt* makes.
Seleucus afterward held *Babylon*,
Antipater, had long rul'd *Macedon*,
These now to govern for the King pretends,
But nothing lesse : each one himself intends.
Perdicas took no Province, like the rest,
But held command o'th' Armies which was best ,
And had a higher project in his head,
Which was his Masters sister for to wed .
So, to the Lady secretly he sent,
That none might know, to frustrate his intent,
But *Cleopatra*, this suitour did deny,
For *Leonatus*, more lovely in her eye,
To whom she sent a message of her mind,
That if he came, good welcome he should find
In these tumultuous dayes, the thralled *Greeks*
Their ancient liberty, afresh now seeks,
Shakes off the yoke, sometimes before laid on
By warlike *Philip*, and his conquering son.
The *Athenians*, force *Antipater* to fly
To *Lamia*, where he shut up doth ly:

To brave *Craterus* then, he sends with speed,
To come and to release him in his need,
The like of *Leonatus*, he requires,
(Which at this time well suited his desires)
For to *Antipater* he now might go,
His Lady take i'th' way, and no man know.
Antiphilus the *Athenian* Generall,
With speed his forces doth together call,
Striving to stop *Leonatus*, that so
He joyn not with *Antipater*, that foe.
The *Athenian* Army was the greater far,
(Which did his match with *Cleopatra* mar)
For fighting still, whilst there did hope remain,
The valiant Chief, amidst his foes was slain,
'Mongst all the Captains of great *Alexander*,
For personage, none was like this Commander :
Now to *Antipater*, *Craterus* goes,
Blockt up in *Lamia*, still by his foes ;
Long marches through *Cilicia* he makes,
And the remains of *Leonatus* takes ,
With them and his, he into *Greece* went,
Antipater releas'd from's prisonment,
After this time, the *Greeks* did never more
Act any thing of worth, as heretofore,
But under servitude, their necks remain'd,
Nor former liberty, or glory gain'd ,
Now dy'd (about the end of th' *Lamian* warre)
Demosthenes, that sweet tongu'd oratour.
Craterus, and *Antipater* now joyn
In love, and in affinity combine:
Craterus doth his daughter *Phila* wed,
Their friendship may the more be strengthened .

Whilst

Whilst they in *Macedon* doe thus agree,
In *Asia* they all asunder be.
Perdicas griev'd, to see the Princes bold,
So many Kingdoms in their power to hold,
Yet to regain them, how he did not know,
For's Souldiers 'gainst those Captains would not goe,
To suffer them goe on, as they begun,
Was to give way, himself might be undone;
With *Antipater* t' joyn, sometimes he thought,
That by his help, the rest might low be brought:
But this again dislikes, and would remain,
If not in word, in deed a Sovraigne.
Desires the King, to goe to *Macedon*,
Which of his Ancestors was once the throne,
And by his presence there, to nullifie
The Acts of his Vice-royes, now grown so high.
Antigonus of Treason first attaints.
And summons him, to answer these complaints,
This he avoyds, and ships himself, and's Son,
Goes to *Antipater*, and tels what's done,
He, and *Craterus*, both with him now joyn,
And gainst *Perdicas*, all their strength combine.
Brave *Ptolomy*, to make a fourth now sent,
To save himself from dangers eminent,
In midst of these, *Garboyles*, with wondrous state,
His Masters Funerals doth celebrate,
At *Alexandria*, in Ægypt Land,
His sumptuous monument long time did stand;
Two years and more since, Natures debt he pai'd,
And yet till now, at quiet was not laid.
Great love did *Ptolomy* by this act gain
And made the Souldiers on his side remain,

Perdi s

Perdicas hears, his foes are now combin'd,
('Gainst which to goe, is trouble in his minde;)
With *Ptolomy* for to begin was best,
Near'st unto him, and farthest from the rest.
Leaves *Eumenes*, the *Asian* coast to free,
From the invasions of the other three,
And with his Army into *Ægypt* goes,
Brave *Ptolomy* to th'utmost to oppose
Perdicas surly carriage, and his pride,
Did alienate the Souldiers from his side;
But *Ptolomy* by affability,
His sweet demeanour, and his courtesie,
Did make his owne firme to his cause remaine,
And from the other, daily some did gaine.
Python, next *Perdicas*, a Captaine high,
Being entreated by him scornfully,
Some of the Souldiers enters *Perdica's* tent,
Knocks out his braines, to *Ptolomy* then went,
And offers him his Honours, and his place,
With stile of the Protector, would him grace;
Next day into the Camp comes *Ptolomy*,
And is of all received joyfully,
Their proffers he refus'd, with modesty
Confers them *Python* on, for's courtesie;
With whom he held, he now was well content,
Then by more trouble to grow eminent
Now comes there newes of a great victor,
That *Eumenes* got of the other three,
Had it but in *Perdicas* life arriv'd,
With greater joy it would have been receiv'd,
Thus *Ptolomy* rich *Ægypt* did retaire,
And *Python* turn'd to *Asia* againe

Whilst

Whilst Perdicas thus staid in Africa,
Antigonus did enter Asis,
And fain would draw Eumenes to their side,
But he alone now faithfull did abide.
The other all, had kingdomes in their eye,
But he was true to's masters family,
Nor could Craterus (whom he much did love)
From his fidelity make him once move.
Two battells now he fought, and had the best,
And brave Craterus slew, amongst the rest,
For this great strife, he pours out his complaints,
And his beloved foe, full sore laments.
I should but snip a story into verse,
And much eclipse his glory to rehearse
The difficulties Eumenes befell,
His stratagems, wherein he did excel,
His policies, how he did extricate
Himself from out of labyrinths intricate.
For all that should be said, let this suffice,
He was both valiant, faithfull, patient, wise.
Python now chose protector of the State,
His rule Queen Euridice begins to hate,
Perceives Arideus must not king it long,
If once young Alexander grow more strong,
But that her Husband serve for supplement,
To warm the seat, was never her intent,
She knew her birthright gave her Macedon,
Grandchild to him, who once sat on that throne,
Who was Perdicas, Philips elder brother,
She daughter to his son, who had no other,
Her mother Cyna sister to Alexander,
Who had an Army, like a great Commander.

C 6 2

Certa the *Phrigian* Queen for to withstand,
And in a Battell flew her hand to hand,
Her Daughter she instructed in that Art,
Which made her now begin to play her part;
Pirhous commands, She ever countermands,
What he appoints, She purposely withstands.
He wearied out, at last, would needs be gone,
Resign'd his place, and so let all alone,
In's stead, the Souldiers chose *Antipater,*
Who vext the Queen more then the other farre;
He plac'd, displac'd, controld, rul'd, as he list,
And this no man durst question, or resist,
For all the Princes of great *Alexander*
Acknowledged for chief, this old Commander.
After a while, to *Macedon* he makes,
The King, and Queen, along with him he takes
Two Sons of *Alexander,* and the rest,
All to be order'd there as he thought best :
The Army with *Antigonus* did leave,
And government of *Asia* to him gave ;
And thus *Antipater* the ground-work layes,
On which *Antigonus* his height doth raise
Who in few years the rest so over-tops,
For universall Monarchy he hopes,
With *Eumenes* he divers Battels fought,
And by his sleights to circumvent him sought,
But vaine it was to use his policy,
'Gainst him, that all deceits could scan, and try.
In this Epitomy, too long to tell
How neatly *Eumenes* did here excell,
That by the selfe same traps the other laid,
He to his cost was righteously repaid.

Now

Now great *Antipater*, the world doth leave
To *Polisperchon*, then his place he gave,
Fearing his Son *Cassander* was unstay'd,
Too young to beare that charge, if on him lay'd ;
Antigonus hearing of his decease,
On most part of *Assyria* doth seize,
And *Ptolomy*, now to encroach begins,
All *Syria*, and, *Phœnicia* he wins ;
Now *Polisperchon* 'gins to act in's place,
Recals *Olimpias*, the Court to grace ;
Antipater had banisht her from thence,
Into *Epire*, for her great turbulence ,
This new Protector's of another minde,
Thinks by her Majesty much help to finde ;
Cassander could not (like his father) see
This *Polisperchons* great ability,
Slights his commands, his actions he disclaimes.
And to be great himselfe now bends his armies ,
Such as his father had advanc'd to place,
Or by his favour any way did grace,
Are now at the devotion of the Son,
Prest to accomplish what he would have done ,
Besides, he was the young Queens favourite,
On whom ('twas thought) she set her chief delight ,
Unto these helps, in *Greece*, he seeks out more,
Goes to *Antigonus*, and doth implore,
By all the Bonds 'twixt him and's father past,
And for that great gift, which he gave him last ,
By these, and all, to grant him some supply,
To take down *Polisperchon* grown so high .
For this *Antigonus* needed no spurs,
Hoping still more to gaine by these new stirs ;

Straight

Straight furnisht him with a sufficient aide,
Cassander for return all speed now made.
Polisperchon, knowing he'd rely
Upon those friends, his father rais'd on high,
Those absent, banished, or else he slew
All such as he suspected to him true.
Cassander with his Hoast to Greece goes,
Whom Polisperchon labours to oppose,
But had the worst at Sea, as well as Land,
And his opponent still got upper hand,
Athens, with many Townes in Greece besides,
Firme to Cassander at this time abides.
Whilst hot in wars these two in Greece remaine,
Antigonus doth all in Asia gaine,
Still labours Eumenes might with him side,
But to the last he faithfull did abide,
Nor could Mother, nor Sons of Alexander,
Put trust in any, but in this Commander,
The great ones now began to shew their minde,
And act, as opportunity they finde.
Aridaeus the second, and simple King,
More then he bidden was, could act no thing,
Polisperchon hoping for's office long,
Thinks to enthrone the Prince when riper grown.
Euridice this injury disdaines,
And to Cassander of this wrong complaines,
Hatefull the Name, and House of Alexander,
Was to this proud, vindicative Cassander,
He still keepeth within his memory,
His Fathers danger, with his Family,
Nor counts he this indignity but small,
When Alexander knockt his head to th' wall.

These

These, with his love, unto the amorous Queen
Did make him vow her servant to be seen.
Olympias, Aride's deadly hates,
As all her Husbands children by his Mates,
She gave him p yson formerly ('tis thought)
Which damage both to minde and body brought :
She now with Polisperchon doth combine,
To make the King by force his seat resigne ;
And her young Nephew in his stead t' inthrone,
That under him she might rule all alone.
For ayde goes to Epire, among her friends,
The better to accomplish these her ends,
Euridice hearing what she intends,
In hast unto her deare Cassander sends,
To leave his Seige at Tegrt, and with speed
To come and succour her, in this great need,
Then by intreaties, promises, and coyne,
Some Forces did procure, with her to joyne.
Olympias now enters Macedon,
The Queen to meet her, bravely marched on,
But when her Souldiers saw their ancient Queen,
Remembring what sometime she had been,
The Wife, and Mother, of their famous Kings,
Nor Darts, nor Arrowes now, none shoots, nor flings,
Then King, and Queen, to Amphipolis doe fly,
But soone are brought into captivity,
The King by extreame torments had his end,
And to the Queen these presents she doth send,
A Halter, cup of Poyson, and a Sword,
Bids chuse her death, such kindnesse sh 'l afford :
The Queen with many a curse, and bitter check,
At length yeel's to the Halter, her faire neck,

                              Praying

Praying, that fatall day might quickly haste,
On which *Olimpias* of the like might taste
This done, the cruell Queen rests not content,
Till all that lov'd *Cassander* was nigh spent,
His Brethren, kinsfolk, and his chiefest friends,
That were within her reach, came to their ends;
Digg'd up his brother dead, 'gainst natures right,
And throwes his bones about, to shew her spight.
The Courtiers wondring at her furious minde,
Wisht in *Epire* she still had been confin'd,
In *Peloponesus* then *Cassander* lay,
Where hearing of this newes he speeds away,
With rage, and with revenge, he's hurried on,
So goes to finde this Queen in *Macedon*,
But being stopt, at Straight *Tharmipoley*
Sea passage gets, and lands in *Thessaly*,
His Army he divides, sends part away,
Polisperchon to hold a while in play,
And with the rest *Olimpias* pursues,
To give her for all cruelties her dues.
She with the flow'r o'th Court to *Pidna* flyes,
Well fortified, and on the Sea it lies,
There by *Cassander* she's block'd up, so long,
Untill the Famine growes exceeding strong,
Her Cousen of *Epire* did what he might,
To raise the Siege, and put her foes to flight,
Cassander is resolv'd, there to remaine,
So succours, and endeavours proves but vaine
Faine would she come now to capitulate,
Cassander will not heare, such is his hate.
The Souldiers pincht with this scarcity,
By stealth unto *Cassander* daily fly,

M

Olimpias

Olimpias wills to keep it, to the last,
Expecting nothing, but of death to taste,
But he unwilling longer there to stay,
Gives promise for her life, and wins the day:
No sooner had he got her in his hands,
But made in Judgement her Accusers stand,
And plead the blood of their deare Kindred spilt,
Desiring Justice might be done for guilt,
And so was he acquitted of his word,
For Justice sake she being put to th' sword.
This was the end of this most cruell Queen,
Whose fury yet unparallela hath been,
The Daughter, Sister, Mother, Wife to Kings,
But Royalty no good conditions brings,
So boundlesse was her pride, and cruelty,
She oft forgot bounds of Humanny.
To Husbands death ('twas thought) she give consent
The Authours death she did so much lament,
With Garlands crown'd his head, bemoin'd his Fates,
His sword unto *Apollo* consecrates:
Her out rages too tedious to relate,
How for no cause, but her inveterate hate;
Her Husbands Wife, and Children, after's death
Some slew, some fry'd, of others, stopt the breath,
Now in her age she's forc't to taste that Cup,
Which she had often made others to sup:
Now many Townes in *Macedon* supprest,
And *Pellas* faine to yeeld amongst the rest,
The Funeralls *Cassandra* celebrates,
Of *Aridaeus*, and his Queen, with state,
Amend their Ancestors by him there laid,
And shewes of lamentati n for them made.

Old

Old *Thebes* he then re built (so much of fame)
And rais'd *Cassandria* after his name, -
But leave him building, others in their urn,
And for a while, let's into *Asia* turn,
True *Eumenes* endeavours by all skill,
To keep *Antigonus* from *Susha* still,
Having Command o'th treasure he can hire,
Such as nor threats, nor favour could acquire,
In divers battels, he had good successe,
Antigonus came off still honourlesse,
When victor oft had been, and so might still,
Penceslas did betray him by a wile,
Antigonus, then takes his life unjust,
Because he never would let go his trust ·
Thus lost he all for his fidelity,
Striving t' uphold h s Masters family,
But as that to a period did haste,
So *Eumenes* of destiny must taste.
Antigonus, all *Persia* now gains,
And Master of the treasure he remains,
Then with *Seleushus* straight at ods doth fall,
But he for aid to *Ptolemy* doth call
The Princes all begin now to envie
Antigorus, his growing up so hye,
Fearing their fate, and what migh. hap ere long,
Enter into a combination strong :
Seleuchus, *Ptolemy*, *Cassander* joynes,
Lysimac'us to make a fourth comb nes.
Antigonue, desirous of the *Greeks*,
To make *Cassander* odious to them, seeks,
Sends forth his declaration from a farre,
And shews what cause they had to take up warre.

The

The Mother of their King to death he'd put,
His Wife, and Son, in prison close had shut,
And how he aymes to make himselfe a King,
And that some title he might seeme to bring,
Thessalonica he had newly wed,
Daughter to *Phillip*, then renowned head,
Had built, and call'd a City by his name,
Which none e're did but those of royall fame,
And in despight of their two famous Kings,
Th' hatefull *Olinthians* to *Greece* re brings,
Rebellious *Thebs* he had re-edified,
Which their late King in dust had damnified,
Requires them therefore to take up their Armes,
And to requite this Traytor for those harmes
Now *Ptolomy* would gaine the Geeks likewise,
For he declares against his injuries,
First, how he held the Empire in his hands,
Seleuchus drove from government, and lands,
Had valiant *Eumenes* unjustly slaine,
And Lord o' th' City *Sushs* did remain
So therefore craves their help to take him down,
Before he weare the universall Crown,
Antigonus at Sea soone had a fight,
Where *Ptol'my*, d the rest put him to flight,
His Son at *Gaza* h' twise left the field,
So *Syria* to *Ptolomy* did yeeld,
And *Seleuchus* recovers *Babylon*,
Still gaining Countries East-ward goes he on
Demetrius againe with *Ptol'omy* did fight,
And comming unawares put him to flight,
But bravely sends the Prisoners back againe,
And all the spoyle and booty they had tane,

Curtius, as noble Ptolomy, or more,
Who at Gaza did th' like to him before
Antigonus did much rejoyce his son,
His lost repute with victorie had won ;
At last these Princes tired out with warres,
Sought for a peace, and laid aside their jarres.
The terms of their agreement thus expresse,
That each shall hold what he doth now possesse,
Till Alexander unto age was grown,
Who then shall be installed in the throne ·
This touch'd Cassander sore, for what he'd done,
Imprisoning both the mother, and her son,
He sees the Greek now favour their young Prince,
Whom he in durance held, now and long since,
That in few years he must be forc'd or glad
To render up such kingdomes as he had
Resolves to quit his fears by one deed done,
And put to death, the mother and her son,
This Roxane for her beautie all commend,
But for one act she did, just was her end,
No sooner was great Alexander dead,
But she Darius's daughters murthered,
Both thrown into a well to hide her blot,
Perdiccas was her partner in this plot.
The Heavens seem'd slow in paying her the same,
But yet at last the hand of vengeance came,
And for that double fact which she had done,
The life of her must go, and of her son
Perdiccas had before, for his amisse,
But from their hands, who thought not once of this.
Cassander's dead, the Princes all detest,
But 'twas in shew, in heart it pleas'd them best

That

That he was odious to the world, they'r glad,
And now they are, free Lords, of what they had,
When this foul tragedy was paſt, and done,
Poliſperchas brings up the other ſon,
Call'd *Hercules*, and elder then his brother,
(But, *Olympias*, thought to preferre th' other:)
The G eeks touch'd with the murther done ſo late,
This Prince began for to compaſſionate
Begin to mutter much 'gainſt proud *Caſſander*,
And place their hopes o'th heire of *Alexander*,
Caſſander fear'd what might of this inſue,
So Po'iſperchen to his Counſell drew,
Gives *Peloponeſus* unto him for hire,
Who ſlew the prince according to deſire:
Thus was the race, and houſe of *Alexander*
Extinct, by this inhumane wretch *Caſſander*,
Antigonus for all this doth not mourn,
He knows to's profit, all i'th end will turn,
But that ſome title he might now pretend,
For marriage to *Cleopatra*, doth ſend
Lyſimachus and *Ptolomy*, the ſame,
And vile *Caſſander* too, ſticks not for ſhame,
She now in *Lydia* at *Sardis* lay,
Where, by Embaſſage, all theſe Princes pray,
Choiſe above all, of *Ptolomy* ſhe makes
With his Embaſſadour, her journey takes,
Antigonus's Lieutenan ſtaves her ſtill,
Untill he further know his Maſters will,
To let her go, er hold her ſtill, he fears,
Antigonus, thus had a wolf by th' ears,
Reſolves at laſt the Princeſſe ſhould be ſlain,
So hinders him of her, he could not gain

Her

Her women are appointed to this deed,
They for their great reward no better speed,
For straight way by command they'r put to death,
As vile consp ratours that took her breath,
And now he thinks, he's ordered all so well,
The wor'd must needs believe what he doth tell :
Thus *Phylips* house was quite extinguished,
Except *Cassanders* wife, who yet not dead,
And by their means, who thought of nothing lesse
Then vengeance just, against the same t' expresse ;
Now blood was pa'd with blood, for what was done
By cruell father, mother, cruell son,
Who did erect their cruelty in guilt,
And wronging innocents whose blood they spilt,
Phylip and *Olimpia*, both were slain,
Arideus and his Queen by slaughters ta'ne ,
Two other children by *Olimpias* kill'd.
And *Cleopatra's* blood, now likewise spili'd,
If *Alexander* was not poysoned,
Yet in the flower of's age, he must lie dead,
His wife and sons then slain by this *Cassander*,
And's kingdomes rent away by each Commander :
Thus may we hear, and say, and ever say,
That hand is righteous still which doth repay ·
These Captains now, the stile of Kings do take,
For to their Crowns, there's none can title make
Demetrius is first, that so assumes,
To do as he, the rest full soon presumes,
To *Athens* then he goes, is entertain'd,
Not like a King, but like some God they fain'd ;
Most grossely base, was this great adulation,
Who incense brent, and offered oblation.

M 4   These

These Kings fall now afresh to warres again,
Demetrius of *Ptolomy* doth gain ,
'Twould be an endlesse story to relate
Their severall battells, and their severall fate,
Antigonus and *Seleuchus*, now fight
Near *Ephesus*, each bringing all their might,
And he that conquerour shall now remain,
Of *Asia* the Lordship shall retain.
This day twixt these two foes ends all the strife,
For here *Antigonus* lost rule, and life,
Nor to his son did there one foot remain,
Of those dominions he did sometimes gain,
Demetrius with his troops to *Athens* flies,
Hoping to find succour in miseries.
But they adoring in prosperity,
Now shut their gates in his adversity,
He sorely griev'd at this his desperate state,
Tries foes, since friends will not compassionate,
His peace he then with old *Seleuchus* makes,
Who his fair daughter *Stratonica* takes,
Antiochus, *Seleuchus* dear lov'd son,
Is for this fresh young Lady half undone,
Falls so extreamly sick, all fear his life,
Yet dares not say he loves his fathers wife ,
When his disease the skilfull Physician found,
He wittily his fathers mind did sound,
Who did no sooner understand the same,
But willingly resign'd the beauteous dame ·
Cassander now must die, his race is run,
And leaves the ill got kingdomes he had won,
Two sons he left, born of King *Philips* daughter,
Who had an end put to their dayes by slaughter

Which

Which should succeed, at variance they fell,
The mother would the youngest should excell,
The eldest enrag'd did play the vipers part,
And with his Sword did pierce his mothers heart,
(Rather then *Philips* child must longer live)
He, whom she gave his life, her death must give)
This by *Lysimachus* soon after slain,
(Whose daughter unto wife, he'd newly ta'n)
The youngest by *Demetrius* kill'd in fight,
Who took away his now preten I'd right
Thus *Philips*, and *Cassander s* race is gone,
And so falls out to be extinct in one,
Yea though *Cassander* died in his bed,
His seed to be extirpt, was destined,
For blood which was decreed, that he should spill,
Yet must his children pay for fathers ill.
Jehu in killing *Ahabs* house did well,
Yet be aveng'd, must th' blood of *Jesreel.*
Demetrius, Cassid rs kingdomes gains,
And now as King, in *Macedon* he reigns,
Seleuchus, Asia holds, that grieves him sore,
Those Countries large, his father got before,
These to recover, musters all his might,
And with his son in law, will needs go fight :
There was he taken and imprisoned
Within an isle that was with pleasures fed,
Injoy'd what so became his Royalty,
Only restrained of his liberty,
After three years he dyed, left what he'd won
In *Greece*, unto *Antigonus*, his son,
For his posterity unto this day,
Did ne'r regain one foot in *Asia*

Now dyed the brave and noble *Ptolomy*,
Renown'd for bounty, valour, clemency,
Rich Ægypt left, and what else he had won
To *Philadelphus*, his more worthy Son
Of the old Heroes, now but two remaine,
Seleuchus and *Lysimachus*, those twaine
Must needs goe try their fortune, and their might,
And so *Lysimachus* was slaine in fight.
'Twas no small joy, unto *Seleuchus* breast,
That now he had out lived all the rest.
Possession he of *Europe* thinks to take,
And so himselfe the only Monarch make,
Whilst with these hopes, in *Greece* he did remaine,
He was by *Ptolomy Ceranus* slaine
The second Son of the first *Ptolomy*,
Who for rebellion unto him did fly,
Seleuchus was as Father, and a friend,
Yet by him had this most unworthy end.
Thus with these Kingly Captaines have we done,
A little now, how the Succession run
Antigonus, *Seleuchus*, and *Cassander*,
With *Ptolomy*, reign'd after *Alexander*,
Cassanders Sons soone after's death were slaine,
So three Successors only did remaine,
Antigonus his Kingdoms lost, and's life,
Unto *Seleuchus*, author of that strife.
His Son *Demetrius*, all *Cassanders* gaines,
And his posterity, the same retaines,
Demetrius Son was call'd *Antigonus*,
And his againe, also *Demetrius*
I must let pass those many battels fought,
Between these Kings, and noble *Pyrrus* stout,

Anl

And his son *Alexander of Epire*,
Whereby immortall honour they acquire
Demetrius had *Philip* to his son,
He *Perseus*, from him th' kingdom's won,
Emillius the *Roman* Generall,
Did take his rule, his sons, himself and all.
This of *Antigonus*, his seed's the fare,
Whose kingdomes were subdu'd by th' *Roman* state.
Longer *Seleu* has held the Royalty
In *Syria* by his posterity,
Antiochus Soter his son was nam'd,
To whom Ancient *Berosus* (so much fam'd)
His book of *Assur* Monarchs dedicates,
Tells of their warres, their names, their riches, fates;
But this is perished with many more,
Which we oft wish were extant as before.
Antiochus Theos was *Soter's* son,
Who a long warre with *Egypt's* King begun.
The affinities and warres *Daniel* set forth,
And calls them there, the Kings of South, and North;
This *Theos* he was murthered by his wife,
Seleuchus reign'd, when he had lost his life,
A third *Seleuchus* next sits on the seat,
And then *Antiochus* surnam'd the great,
Seleucus next *Antiochus* succeeds,
And then *Epiphanes*, whose wicked deeds,
Horrid massacres, murders, cruelties,
Against the Jewes we read in *Machabees*,
By him was set up the abomination
I th' holy place, which caused desolation,
Antiochus Eupator was the next,
By Rebells and imposters daily vext,

So

So many Princes still were murthered,
The Royall blood was quite extinguished.
That *Tygranes* the great *Armenian* King,
To take the government was called in,
Him *Lucullus*, the *Romane* Generall
Vanquish'd in fight, and took those kingdomes all,
Of *Greece*, and *Syria* thus the rule did end,
In *Egypt* now a little time we I spend.
First *Ptolomy* being dead, his famous son,
Cal'd *Philadelphus*, next sat on the throne,
The Library at *Alexandria* built,
With seven hundred thousand volumes fill'd,
The seventy two interpreters did seek,
They might translate the Bible into *Greek*,
His son was *Evergetes* the last Prince
That valour shew'd, vertue or excellence.
Philopater was *Evergete's* son.
After *Epiphanes*, sat on the Throne
Philometer, then *Evergetes* again
And next to him, did false *Lathurus* reigne,
Alexander, then *Lathurus* in's stead,
Next *Auletes*, who cut off *Pompey's* head
To all these names we *Ptolomy* must adde,
For since the first, that title still they had,
Fair *Cleopatra* next, last of that race,
Whom *Julius Cæsar* set in Royall place,
Her brother by him, lost his trayterous head
For *Pompey's* life, then plac'd her in his stead,
She with her Paramour *Mark Antony*,
Held for a time the *Egyptian* Monarchy.
Till great *Augustus* had with him a fight,
At *Actium* stair, his Navy put to flight.

Then

Then poysonous Aspes she sets unto her Armes,
T take her life, and quit her from all harmes ;
For 'twas not death, nor danger, she did dread,
But some disgrace, in triumph to be led
Here ends at last the *Grecian* Monarchy,
Which by the *Romans* had its destiny
Thus Kings, and Kingdoms, have then times, and dates,
Their standings, over-turnings, bounds, and fates ;
Now up, now down, now chief, and then brought under ,
The Heavens thus rule, to fit the earth with wonder
The *Assyrian* Monarchy long time did stand,
But yet the *Persian* got the upper hand ,
The *Grecian*, them did utterly subdue,
And Millions were subjected unto few :
The *Grecian* longer then the *Persian* stood,
Then came the *Romane*, like a raging flood,
And with the torrent of his rapid course,
Their Crownes, their Titles, riches beares by force.
The first, was likened to a head of gold,
Next, armes and breast, of silver to behold ,
The third, belly and thighs of brasse in sight,
And last was Iron, which breaketh all with might.
The Stone out of the Mountaine then did rise,
And smote those feet, those legs, those arms and thighs;
Then gold, silver, brasse, iron, and all that store,
Became like chaffe upon the threshing floor ,
The first a Lyon, second was a Beare,
The third a Leopard, which four wings did beare ,
The last more strong, and dreadfull, then the rest,
Whose Iron teeth devoured every beast,
And when he had no appetite to eate,
The residue he stamped under s feet .

                                    Bur

But yet this Lion, Bear, this Leopard, Ram,
All trembling stand, before that powerfull Lambe.
With these three Monarchies, now have I done,
But how the fourth, their Kingdoms from them won;
And how from small beginnings it did grow,
To fill the world with terrour, and with woe:
My tired braine, leaves to a better pen,
This taske befits not women, like to men:
For what is past I blush, excuse to make,
But humbly stand, some grave reproof to take:
Pardon to crave, for errours, is but vaine,
The Subject was too high, beyond my straine;
To frame Apologie for some offence,
Converts our boldnesse, into impudence.
This my presumption (some now) to requite,
Ne futer ultra crepidum, may write.

A Fter some dayes of rest, my restlesse heart,
To finish what began, new thoughts impart
And maugre all resolves, my fancy wrought
This fourth to th' other three, now might be brought.
Shortnesse of time, and inability,
Will force me to a confus'd brevity;
Yet in this Chaos, one shall easily spy,
The vast limbs of a mighty Monarchy.
What e're is found amisse, take in best part,
As faults proceeding from my head, not heart.

The

The *Roman* Monarchy,
being the Fourth, and last,
beginning, *Anno Mundi,*
3 2 1 3.

Tout *Romulus,* *Romes* Founder, and first
King,
Whom vestall *Rhea,* into th' world did
bring
His Father was not *Mars,* as some devis'd,
But *Æmulus,* in Armour all disguis'd
Thus he deceiv'd his Neece, she might not know
The double injury, he then did doe:
Where Shepheards once had Coats, and Sheep their
Folds,
Where Swines, and rustick Peasants made their
Holds.
A Citty faire did *Remulus* erect
The Mistris of the World, in each respect.
His Brother *Remus* there, by him was slaine,
For leaping o're the Walls with some disdaine;
The Stones at first was cimented with bloud,
And bloudy hath it prov'd, since first it stood:

This

This City built, and Sacrifices done,
A forme of Government he next begun ;
A hundred Senators he likewise chose,
And with the stile of *Patres* honour'd those,
His City to replenish, men he wants,
Great priviledges then, to all he grants,
That wil within these strong built walls reside,
And this new gentle Government abide :
Of Wives there was so great a scarsity,
They to their neighbours sue, for a supply ;
But all disdaine alliance then to make,
So *Romulus* was forc'd this course to take.
Great shewes he makes at Tilt, and Turnament,
To see these sports, the *Sabins* all are bent ;
Their Daughters by the *Romans* then were taught,
For to recover them, i'Feild was fought ;
But in the end, to finall peace they come,
And *Sabins*, as one people, dwelt in *Rome*.
The *Romans* now more potent 'gin to grow,
And *Fedinates* they wholly over-throw.
But *Romulus* then comes unto his end,
Some faining say, to heav'n he did ascend,
Others, the seven and thirtyeth of his reigne
Affirme, that by the Senate he was slaine.

Numa Pompilius.

Numa *Pompilius*, is next chosen King,
Held for his Piety, some sacred thing ;
To *Janus*, he that famous Temple built,
Kept shut in peace, but ope when blond was spi't,
Religious

Religious Rites, and Customs instituted,
And Priests, and Flamines likewise he deputed ;
Their Augurs strange, their habit, and attire,
And vestall Maids to keep the holy fire.
Goddesse *Ægeria* this to I am told,
So to delude the people he was bold :
Forty three yeares he rul'd with generall praise.
Accounted for some god in after dayes.

Tullus Hostilius.

Tullus Hostilius, was third Roman King,
Who Martiall Discipline in use did bring ;
War with the antient *Albans* he doth wage,
The strife to end, six Brothers doe ingage ;
Three call'd *Horatii*, on *Romes* side,
And *Curiatii*, three *Albans* provide ,
The *Romans* Conquereth, others yeeld the day,
Yet for their compact, after false they play :
The *Romans* sore incens'd, their Generall slay,
And from old *Alba* fetch the wealth away ;
Of *Latine* Kings this was long since the Seat,
But now demolished, to make *Rome* great
Thirty two years doth *Tullus* reigne, then dye,
Leaves *Rome*, in wealth and power, still growing high.

Ancus Martius.

Next, *Ancus Martius* sits upon the Throne,
Nephew unto *Pompilius* dead, and gone ,

N

Rome

Rome he inlarg'd, new builte againe the wall,
Much stronger, and more beautifull withall ;
A stately Bridge he over *Tyber* made,
Of Boats, and Oires, no more they need the aide
Faire *Ostia* he built, this Towne, it stood,
Close by the mouth of famous *Tyber* flood :
Twenty foure yeare, th' time of his royall race,
Then unto death unwillingly gives place.

Tarquinius Priscus.

TArquin, a Greek, at *Corinth* borne, and bred,
Who for sedition from his Country fled,
Is entertain'd at *Rome*, and in short time,
By wealth, and favour, doth to honour climbe ;
He after *Martius* death the Kingdome had,
A hundred Senatours he more did adde ,
Warres with the *Latins* he againe renewes,
And Nations twelve, of *Tuscary* subdues :
To such rude triumphs, as young *Rome* then had,
Much state, and glory, did this *Priscus* adde .
Thirty eight yeares (this Stranger borne) did reigne,
And after all, by *Ancus* Sons was slaine

Sextus Tullius.

NExt, *Sextus Tullius* his upon the Throne,
Ascends not up, by merits of his owne ,
but by the favour, and the speciall grace
Of *Tanaquil*, the Queen, obtaines the place ;

He

He ranks the people, into each degree,
As wealth had made them of abilitie ;
A generall Muster takes, which by account,
To eighty thousand soules then did amount :
Forty foure yeares did *Servius Tullius* reigne,
And then by *Tarquin, Priscus* Son, was slaine.

Tarquinius Superbus, the last *Roman* King.

TArquin the proud, from manners called so,
Sate on the Throne, when he had slaine his foe ;
Sextus his Son, doth (most unworthily)
Lucretia's force, mirrour of chastity ,
She loathed so the fact, she loath'd her life,
And shed her guiltlesse blood, with guilty knife
Her Husband sore incens'd, to quit this wrong,
With *Junius Pratus* rose, and being strong,
The *Tarquins* they from *Rome* with speed expell,
In banishment perpetuall, to dwell ,
The Government they change, a new one bring,
And people sweare, ne're to accept of King.

The end of the Roman Monarchy,
being the fourth and last.

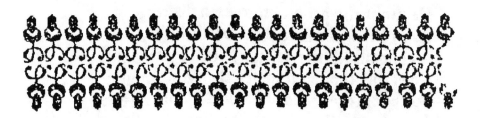

A Dialogue between Old

England and New, concern-
ing their prefent troubles.
Anno 1 6 4 2.

New England.

Las, deare Mother, faireft Queen, and beft,
With honour, wealth, and peace, happy and
bleft,
What ayles thee hang thy head, and croffe
thine armes ?
And fit i'th duft, to figh thefe fad alarms ?
What deluge of new woes thus over whelme
The glories of thy ever famous Realme ?
What meanes this wailing tone, this mourning guife ?
Ah, tell thy Daughter ; fhe may fimpathize.

Old England.

Art ignorant indeed, of thefe my woes ?
Or muft my forced tongue thefe griefes difclofe ?

And

And muſt my ſelfe diſſect my tatter'd ſtate,
  Which 'mazed Chriſtendome ſtands wondring at?
And thou a childe, a Limbe, and doſt not feele
My weakned fainting body now to reele?
This Phiſick-purging-potion I have taken,
Will bring Conſumption, or an Ague quaking,
Unleſſe ſome Cordial thou fetch from high,
Which preſent help may eaſe this malady
If I deceaſe, doſt think thou ſhalt ſurvive?
Or by my waſting ſtate, doſt think to thrive?
  Then weigh our caſe, if't be not juſtly ſad,
Let me lament alone, while thou art glad

New England.

And thus, alas, your ſtate you much deplore,
In generall terms, but will not ſay wherefore:
What Medicine ſhall I ſeek to cure this woe.
If th' wound's ſo dangerous I may not know?
But you perhaps would have me gueſſe it out,
What, hath ſome *Herod*, like that *S-raſh*out,
By fraud, and force, uſurp'd thy flowing crown,
And by tempeſtuous Wars thy fields trod down?
O hath *Canutus*, that brave valiant *Dane*,
The regall, peacefull Scepter from thee tane?
Or is't a *Norman*, whoſe victorious hand
With *Engliſh* blood bedews thy conquered Land?
Or is't inteſtine Wars that thus offend?
Doe *Maud*, and *Stephen* for the Crown contend?
Doe Barons riſe, and ſide againſt their King?
And call in Forreign ayde to help the thing?

Muſt

Muſt *Edward* be depos'd, or is't the houre
That ſecond *Richard* muſt be clapt i'th' Tower?
Or is the fatall jarre againe begun,
That from the red, white pricking Roſes ſprung?
Muſt *Richmonds* ayd, the Nobles now implore,
To come, and break the tuſhes of the Boar?
If none of theſe, deare Mother, what's your woe?
Pray, doe not feare *Spaines* bragging Armado?
Doth your Allye, faire *France*, conſpire your wrack?
Or, doth the *Scots* play falſe behind your back?
Doth *Holland* quit you ill, for all your love?
Whence is this ſtorme, from Earth, or Heaven above?
Is't Drought, is't Famine, or is't Peſtilence?
Doſt feele the ſmart, or feare the conſequence?
Your humble Childe intreats you, ſhew your grief,
Though Armes, nor Purſe ſhe hath, for your releif:
Such is her poverty, yet ſhall be found
A ſupplyant for your help, as ſhe is bound.

Old England.

I muſt confeſſe, ſome of thoſe Sores you name,
My beauteous Body at this preſent maime,
But forraigne Foe, nor fained friend I feare,
For they have work enough (thou knowſt) elſewhere,
Nor is it *Alcies* Son, and *Berries* Daughter,
Whoſe proud contention cauſe this ſlaughter,
Nor Nobles ſiding, to make *John* no King
French *Lewis* unjuſtly to the Crown to bring;
No *Edward, Richard*, to loſe rule, and life,
Nor no *Lancaſtrians*, to renew old ſtrife;

No

No Crook backt Tyrant, now ufurps the Seat,
  Whofe tearing tusks did wound, and kill, and threat:
  Duke of *York*, nor Earle of *March*, to foyle
Their hands, in Kindreds blood, whom they did foyle:
No need of *Teder*, Rofes to unite,
None knowes which is the Red, or which the White:
Spaines braving Fleet a fecond time is funke,
France knowes, how of my fury fhe hath drunk,
By Edward third, and *Henry* fifth of fame,
Her Lillies in mine Armes avouch the fame.
My Sifter *Scotland* hurts me now no more,
Though fhe hath bin injurious heretofore.
What *Holland* is, I am in fome fufpence,
But truft not much unto his Excellence,
For wants, fure fome I feele, but more I feare,
And for the Pestilence, who knowes how neare:
Famine, and Plague, two fifters of the Sword,
Deftruction to a Land doth foone afford,
They're for my punifhments ordain'd on high,
Unleffe thy teares prevent it fpeedily.
But yet, I anfwer not what you demand,
To fhew the grievance of my troubled Land,
Before I tell the effect, ile fhew the caufe,
Which are my Sins, the breach of facred Lawes,
Idolatry, fupplanter of a Nation,
With foolifh fuperftitious adoration;
And lik'd, and countenanc'd by men of might,
The Gofpel is trod down, and hath no right,
Church Offices are fold, and bought, for gaine,
That Pope, had hope, to finde *Rome* here againe,
For Oathes, and Blafphemies did ever eare
From *Beelzebub* himfelf, fuch language heare?

N 4   What

What scorning of the Saints of the most high,
What injuries did daily on them lye;
What false reports, what nick-names did they take,
Not for their owne, but for their Masters sake;
And thou, poore soule, wast jeer'd among the rest,
Thy flying for the Truth I'made a jeast,
For Sabbath-breaking, and for Drunkennesse,
Did ever Land prophannesse more expresse?
From crying bloods, yet cleansed am not I,
Martyrs, and others, dying causelesly:
How many Princely heads on blocks laid down,
For nought, but title to a fadin   Crown?
'Mongst all the cruelties which   have done,
Oh, *Edwards* Babes, and *Clarence* haplesse Son,
O *Jane*, why didst thou dye in flowring prime,
Because of Royall Stem, that was thy crime.
For Bribery, *Adultery*, for Thefts, and Lyes,
Where is the *Nation*, I cann'epraiize;
With Usury, Extortion, and Oppression,
These be the *Hydra*'s of my stout transgression,
These be the bitter fountains, heads, and runts,
Whence flow'd the source, the sprigs, the boughs, and
Of more then thou canst heare, or I relate,   (fruits,
That with high hand I still did perpetrate,
For these, were threatned the wofull day,
I mock'd the Preachers, put it faire away,
The Sermons yet upon record doe stand,
That cry'd, destruction to my wicked Land:
These Prophets mouthes (alas the while) was stopt,
Unworthily, some backs whipt, and eares cropt;
Their reverent cheeks, did beare the glorious markes
Of sinking, stigmatizing, Romish Clerkes,

                                        Some

Some loft their livings, fome in prifon pent,
  ſome groſſely fin'd, from friends to exile went :
Their ſilent tongues to heaven did vengeance cry,
Who heard their cauſe, and wrongs judg'd righteouſly,
And will repay it ſevenfold in my lap,
This is fore-runner of my after clap,
Nor took I warning by my neighbours falls,
I ſaw ſad *Germanie's* diſmantled walls.
I ſaw her people famiſh'd, Nobles ſlain,
Her fruitfull land, à barren heath remain
I ſaw (unmov'd) her Armies, foil'd and fled,
Wives fore'd, babes toſs'd, her houſes calcined,
I ſaw ſtrong *Rochel* yeelding to her foe,
Thouſands of ſtarved Chriſtians there alſo.
I ſaw poore *Ireland* bleeding out her laſt, ⎰
Such cruelty as all reports have paſt ⎱
My heart obdurate, ſtood not yet aghaſt
Now ſip I of that cup, and juſt 't may be,
The bottome dregs reſerved are for me.

New England.

To all you've ſaid, ſad mother, I aſſent
Your fearfull ſinnes, great cauſe there's to lament,
My guilty hands (in part) hold up with you,
A ſharer in your puniſhment's my due,
But all you ſay, amounts to this effect,
Not what you feel, but what you do expect.
Pray in plain termes, what is your preſent grief,
Then let's join heads, and hands for your relief.

Old

Old England.

Well, to the matter then, there's grown of late,
'Twixt King and Peeres a question of state,
Which is the chief, the law, or else the King,
One saith its he, the other no such thing
My better part in Court of Parliament,
To ease my groaning land shew their intent,
To crush the proud, and right to each man deal
To help the Church, and stay the Common-Weal,
So many obstacles comes in their way,
As puts me to a stand what I should say,
Old customes, new Prerogatives stood on,
Had they not held law fast, all had been gone,
Which by their prudence stood them in such stead,
They took hugh *Strafford* lower by the head,
And to their *Laud* be't spoke, they held i'th' Tower,
All *Englands* Metropolitane that houre,
This done, an Act they would have passed fain,
No prelate should his Bishoprick retain,
Here rugg'd they hard indeed, for all men saw,
This must be done by *Gospel*, not by law
Next the *Militia* they urged sore,
This was deny'd, I need not say *wherefore*
The King displeas'd, at *York* himself absents.
They humbly beg return, shew their intents,
The writing, printing, posting to and fro,
Shews all was done, I'll therefore let it go
But now I come to speak of my disaster,
Contention's grown 'twixt Subjects and their Master

They

They worded it so long, they fell to blows,
That thousands lay on heaps, here bleeds my woes.
I that no warres, so many yeares have known,
Am now destroy'd, and slaughter'd by mine own,
But could the field alone this cause decide,
One battell, two or three I might abide,
But these may be beginnings of more woe,
Who knows, the worst, the best may overthrow,
Religion, Gospell, here lies at the stake,
Pray now dear child, for sacred *Zions* sake,
Oh pity me, in this sad perturbation,
My plundered *Townes*, my houses devastation,
My ravisht virgins, and my young men slain,
My wealthy trading fln, my dearth of grain,
The seed time's come, but Ploughman hath no hope,
Because he knows not, who shall inn his crop:
The poore they want their pay, their children bread,
Their wofull mother's tears unpitied.
If any pity in thy heart remain,
Or any child-like love thou dost retain,
For my relief now use thy utmost skill,
And recompence me good, for all my ill

New England.

Dear mother cease complaints, and wipe your eyes,
Shake off your dust, chear up, and now arise,
You are my mother, nurse, I once your flesh,
Your sunken bowels gladly would refresh:
Your griefs I pity much, but should do wrong,
To weep for that we both have pray'd for long,

To

To see these latter dayes of hop'd for good,
That Right may have its right, though 't be with blood,
After dark Popery the day did clear,
But now the Sun in's brightnesse shall appear,
Blest be the Nobles of thy Noble Land,
With (ventur'd lives) for truths defence that stand,
Blest be thy Commons, who for Common good,
And thine infringed Lawes have boldly stood
Blest be thy Counties which do aid thee still
With hearts and states, to testifie their will.
Blest be thy Preachers, who do chear thee on,
O cry the sword of God, and *Gideon*.
And shall I not on those with *Meroz's* curse,
That help thee not with prayers, armes, and purse,
And for my self, let miseries abound,
If mindlesse of thy state I e'r be found
These are the dayes, the Churches foes to crush,
To root out Prelates, head, tail, branch, and rush.
Let s bring *Baals* vestments out, to make a fire,
Their Myters, Surplices, and all their tire,
Copes, Rochets, Crossiers, and such trash,
And let their names consume, but let the flash
Light Christendome, and all the world to see,
We hate *Romes* Whore, with all her trumperie.
Go on brave *Essex*, shew whose son thou art,
Not false to King, nor Countrey in thy heart,
But those that hurt his people and his Crown,
By force expell, destroy, and tread them down.
Let Gioles be fill'd with th'remainer of that pack
And sturdy *Tyburn* loaded till it crack,
And yee brave Nobles, chase away all fear,
And to this blessed Cause close's adhere

O

mother, can you weep, and have such Peeres.
When they are gone, then drown your self in teares.
If now you weep so much, that then no more,
The briny Ocean will o'reflow your shore,
These, these, are they (I trust) with *Charles* our King,
Out of all mists, such glorious dayes will bring,
That dazzled eyes beholding much shall wonder
At that thy setled Peace, thy wealth and splendour,
Thy Church and Weal, establish'd in such manner,
That all shall joy that thou display'dst thy banner,
And discipline erected, so I trust,
That nursing Kings, shall come and lick thy dust.
Then Justice shall in all thy Courts take place,
Without respect of persons, or of case,
Then bribes shall cease, and suits shall not stick long,
Patience, and purse of Clients for to wrong
Then High Commissions shall fall to decay,
And Pursevants and Catchpoles want their pay,
So shall thy happy Nation ever flourish,
When truth and righteousnesse they thus shall nourish
When thus in Peace, thine Armies brave send out,
To such proud *Rome*, and all her vassalls rout
There let thy name, thy fame, thy valour shine,
As did thine Ancestours in *Palestine*,
And let her spoils, full pay, with int'rest be,
Of what unjustly once she poll'd from thee,
Or all the woes thou canst let her be sped,
Execute to th' full the vengeance threatned.
Bring forth the beast that rul'd the world with's beck,
And tear his flesh, and set your feet on's neck,
And make his filthy den so desolate,
To th' astonishment of all that knew his state,

I i   l

This done, with brandish'd swords, to *Turky* go,
(For then what is't, but English blades dare do)
And lay her waft, for so's the facred doom,
And do to *Gog*, as thou haft done to *Rome.*
Oh *Abrahams* feed lift up your heads on high
For fure the day of your redemption's nigh,
The fcales fhall fall from your long blinded eyes
And him you fhall adore, who now defpife,
Then fulnes of the Nations in fhall flow,
And Jew and Gentile, to one worfhip go,
Then follows dayes of happineffe and reft,
Whofe lot doth fall to live therein is bleft :
No Canaanite fhall then be found ith' land,
And holineffe, on horfes bells fhall ftand,
If this make way thereto, then figh no more,
But if at all, thou didft not fee't before.
Farewell dear mother, Parliament, prevail,
And in a while you'l tell another tale

An Elegie upon that Honourable and renowned Knight,

Sir *Philip Sidney*, who was untimely slaine at the Seige of *Zutphon*,
Anno 1 5 8 6

By *A. B.* in the yeare, 1638.

When *England* did injoy her Halfion dayes,
   Her noble *Sidney* were the Crown of Bayes;
No lesse an Honour to our *British* Land,
Then she that sway'd the Scepter with her hand ·
Mars and *Minerva* did in one agree,
Of Armes, and Arts, thou should'st a patterne be.
Calliope with *Terpsecher* did sing,
Of Poesie and of Musick thou wert King,
Thy Rhethorick it struck *Polimnia* dead,
Thine Eloquence made *Mercury* wax red,
Thy Logick from *Euterpe* won the Crown,
More worth was thine, then *Clio* could set down
Thalia and *Melpomene* say th' truth,
(Witnesse *Arcadia*, penn'd in his youth)

                         Arc

Are not his Tragick Comedies so acted,
As if your nine-fold wit had been compacted;
To shew the wold, they never saw before,
That this one Volumne should exhaust your store,
I praise thee not for this, it is unfit,
This was thy shame, O miracle of wit:
Yet doth thy shame (with all) purchase renown,
What doe thy very is then ? Oh, honours crown l
In all records, thy Name I ever see,
Put with an Epithet of dignity;
Which shewes, thy worth was great, thine honour such,
The love thy Country ought thee, was as much.
Let then, none dis-allow of these my straines,
Which have the self same blood yet in my veines;
Who honours thee for what was honourable,
But leaves the rest, as most unprofitable:
Thy wiser dayes, condemn'd thy witty works,
Who knowes the Spels that in thy Rethorick lurks?
But some infatuate fooles soone caught therein,
Found Cupids Dam, had never such a Gin,
Which makes severer eyes but scorn thy Story,
And modest Maids, and Wives, blush at thy glory;
Yet, he's a beetle head, that cann't discry
A world of treasure, in that rubbish lye,
And doth thy selfe, thy worke, and honour wrong,
(O brave Refiner of our British Tongue;)
That sees not learning, valour, and morality,
Justice, friend'ship, and kind hospitality;
Yea, and Divinity within thy Book,
Such were prejudicate and did not look:
But to say truth, thy worth I shall but staine,
Thy fame, and praise, is farre beyond my straine,

Yet

Yet great *Augustus* was content (we know)
To be saluted by a filly Crow ;
Then let fuch Crowes as I, thy praifes fing,
A Crow's a Crow, and *Cæſar* is a King.
O brave *Achilles*, I wifh fome *Homer* would
Engrave on Marble, in characters of Gold,
What famous feats thou didſt,on *Flanders* coaſt,
Of which, this day, faire *Belgia* doth boaſt.
O *Zutphon*, *Zutphon*, that moſt fatall City,
Made famous by thy fall, much more's the pitty;
Ah, in his blooming prime, death pluckt this Rofe,
E're he was ripe ; his thred cut *Atropos*.
Thus man is borne to dye, and dead is he,
Brave *Hector* by the walls of *Troy*, we fee :
Oh, who was neare thee, but did fore repine ;
He refcued not with life, that life of thine,
But yet impartiall Death this Boone did give,
Though *Sidney* dy'd, his valiant name ſhould live ;
And live it doth, in fpight of death, through fame,
Thus being over-come, he over-came.
Where is that envious tongue, but can afford,
Of this our noble *Scipio* fome good word ?
Noble *Bartas*, this to thy praife adds more,
In fad, fweet verfe, thou didſt his death deplore ;
Illuſtrious *Stella*, thou didſt thine full well,
If thine afpect was milde to *Aſtrophill* ,
I feare thou wert a Commet, did portend
Such prince as he, his race ſhould ſhortly end :
If fuch Stars as thefe, fad prefages be,
I wifh no more fuch Blazers we may fee ;
But thou art gone, fuch Meteors never laſt.
And as thy beauty, fo thy name would waſt,

O   But

But that it is record by *Philips* hand,
That such an omen once was in our land',
O Princely *Philip*, rather *Alexander*,
Who wert of honours band, the chief Commander.
How could that *Stella*, so confine thy will?
To wait till she, her influence distill,
I rather judg'd thee of his mind that wept,
To be within the bounds of one world kept,
But *Omphala*, see *Hercules* to spin,
And *Mars* himself was ta'n by *Venus* gin;
Then wonder lesse, if warlike *Philip* yield,
When such a *Hero* shoots him out o'th' field,
Yet this preheminence thou hast above,
That thine was true, but theirs adult'rate love
Fain would I shew, how thou fame's path didst tread,
But now into such Lab'rinths am I led
With endlesse turnes, the way I find not out,
For to persist, my muse is more in doubt.
Calls me ambitious fool, that durst aspire,
Enough for me to look, and so admire
And makes me now with *Sylvester* confesse,
But *Sydney's* Muse, can sing his worthinesse.
Too late my errour see, that durst presume
To fix my faltering lines upon his tomb
Which are no worth, as far short of his due,
As I u can is, of *Venus* native hue
Goodwill, did make my head-long pen to run,
Like unwise *Phae* on his ill guided sonne,
Till taught to's cost, for his too lusty hand,
He left that charge by *Phoebus* to be man'd
So proudly foolish I, with *Phaeton* strive,
Fame's flaming Chariot for to drive.

Till

Till terrour-struck for my too weighty charge.
I leave't in brief, *Apollo* do't at large.
Apollo laught to patch up what's begun,
He bad me drive, and he would hold the Sun ;
Better my hap, then was his darlings fate,
For dear regard he had of *Sydney's* state,
Who in his Deity, had so deep share,
That those that name his fame, he needs must spare,
He promis'd much, but th' muses had no will,
To give to their detractor any quill.
With high disdain ,they said they gave no more,
Since *Sydney* had exhausted all their store,
That this contempt it did the more perplex,
In being done by one of their own sex ,
They took from me, the scribling pen I had,
I to be eas'd of such a task was glad.
For to revenge his wrong, themselves ingage,
And drave me from *Parnassus* in a rage,
Not because, sweet *Sydney's* fame was not dear,
But I had blemish'd theirs, to make 't appear :
I pensive for my fault, sat down, and then,
Errata, through their leave threw me my pen,
I or to conclude my poem two lines they daigne,
Which writ, she bad return't to them again.
So *Sidney's* fame, I leave to *England's* Rolls,
His bones do lie inter'd in stately *Pauls.*

His Epitaph.

Here lies intomb'd in fame,under this stone,
Philip and Alexander both in one.

Here

Here to the Muſes, the Son of Mars in truth,
Learning, valour, beauty, all in vertuous youth
His praiſe is much, this ſhall ſuffice my pen,
That Sidney dy'd the quinteſſence of men

In honour of *Du Bartas.*
1 6 4 1.

A. B.

AMongſt the happy wits this Age hath ſhowne,
   Great, deare, ſweet *Bartas*, thou art matchleſſe
      knowne ;
My raviſht eyes, and heart, with faltering tongue,
In humble wiſe have vow'd their ſervice long,
But knowing th' taske ſo great, and ſtrength but ſmall,
Gave o're the work, before begun withall :
My dazled ſight of late, review'd thy lines,
Where Art, and more then Art in Nature ſhines,
Reflection from their beaming altitude,
Did thaw my frozen hearts ingratitude ;
Which Rayes, darting upon ſome richer ground,
Had cauſed flowers, and fruits, ſoone to abound ,
But barren I, my Dayſey here doe bring,
A homely flower in this my latter ſpring .
If Summer, or my Autumne age, doe yeeld
Flowers, fruits, in garden, orchard, or in field ,
                    They

They shall be consecrated in my Verse,
And proftrate oft'red at great *Bartas* Herfe
My Mufe unto a Childe, I firly may compare,
Who fees the riches of fome furious Fayre,
He feeds his eyes, but underftanding lacks,
To comprehend the worth of all thofe knicks,
The glittering Plate, and Jewels, he admires,
The Hits, and fans, the Plumes, and Ladies tires,
And thoufand times his mared minde doth wifh
Some part, at leaft, of that brave wealth was his,
But feeing empty wifhes nought obtaine,
At night returns to his Mothers cot againe,
And tells her tales, (his full heart over-glad)
Of all the glorious fights his eyes have had :
But findes too foone his want of Eloquence,
The filly Pratler fpeakes no word of fenfe;
And feeing utterance fayle his great defires,
Sits down in filence, deeply he admires
Thus weake brain'd I, reading thy lofty ftile,
Thy profound Learning, viewing other while
Thy Art in Naturall Philofophy.
Thy Saint-like minde in grave Divinity,
Thy peircing skill in high Aftronomy,
And curious in-fight in Anatomy,
Thy Phifick, Mufick, and State policy,
Valour in War, in Peace good Husbandry,
Sure liberall Nature, did with Art not fmall,
In all the Arts make thee moft liberall,
A thou'and thoufand times my fenfleffe Sences,
Moveleffe, ftand charm'd by thy fweet influences,
More fenceleffe then the Stones to *Amphions* Lute,
Mine eyes are fightleffe, and my tongue is mute,

My

My full aftonifh'd heart doth pant to break,
Through grief it wants a faculty to fpeak,
Vollies of praifes could I eccho then,
Had I an Angels voice, or *Bartas*'s pen,
But wifhes cann't accomplifh my defire,
Pardon, if I adore, when I admire
O *France*, in him thou didft more glory gain,
Then in thy *Pippin, Martell, Charlemain*.
Then in Saint *Lewis*, or thy laft *Henry* great,
Who tam'd his foes, in bloud, in fkarres and fweat,
Thy fame is fpread as farre, I dare be bold,
In all the Zones, the temp'rate, hot and cold,
Their trophies were but heaps of wounded flain,
Thine the quinteffence of an Heroick brain.
The Oaken garland ought to deck their browes,
Immortall bayes, all men to thee allows.
Who in thy tryumphs (never won by wrongs)
Leadft millions chaind by eyes, by eares, by tongues,
Oft have I wond'red at the hand of heaven,
In giving one, what would have ferved feven.
If e'r this golden gift was fhowr'd on any,
Thy double portion would have ferved many.
Unto each man his riches are affign'd,
Of names, of ftate, of body, or of mind,
Thou haft thy part of all, but of the laft,
Oh pregnant brain, Oh comprehenfion vaft,
Thy haughty ftile, and rapted wit fublime,
All ages wondring at, fhall never clime
Thy facred works are not for imitation,
But monuments for future admiration :
Thus *Bartas* fame fhall laft while ftarres do ftand,
And whilft there's aire, or fire, or fea or land

But

But left my ignorance should doe thee wrong,
To celebrate thy merits in my Song,
Ile leave thy praife, to thofe shall doe thee right,
Good will, not skill, did caufe me bring my mite.

His Epitaph.

HEre lyes the pearle of France, Parnaffus glory,
The world rejoic'd at's birth, at's death was forry,
Art and Nature joyn'd, by heavens high decree,
Now shew'd what once they ought, Humanity,
And Natures Law, had it been revocable,
To refcue him from death, Art had been able:
But Nature vanquifh'd Art, fo Bartas dy'd,
But Fame out living both, he is reviv'd.

✿✿✿✿✿✿✿✿✿✿✿✿✿✿✿✿✿✿✿✿✿✿✿✿✿

In honour of that High and Mighty Princefs, Queen ELIZABETH, of moft happy memory.

The Proem.

ALthough great Queen, thou now in filence lye,
Yet thy loud Herauld Fame, doth to the sky
Thy wondrous worth proclaime, in every clime,
And fo has vow'd, whilft there is world, or time,

So great's thy glory, and thine excellence,
The sound thereof raps every humane sence ;
That men account it no impiety,
To say, thou wert a fleshly Deity :
Thousands bring off'rings, (though out of date)
Thy world of honours to accumulate,
Mongst hundred Hecatombs of roaring Verse,
'Mine bleating stands before thy royall Herse
Thou never didst, nor canst thou now disdaine,
T' accept the tribute of a loyall Braine ,
Thy clemency did ferst esteeme as much
The acclamations of the poore, as rich ;
Which makes me deeme, my rudenesse is no wrong,
Though I resound thy greatnesse 'mongst the throng.

The Poem.

NO *Phœnix* Pen, nor *Spencers* Poetry,
No *Speeds*, nor *Chamdens* learned History,
Eliza's works, wars, praise, can e're compact,
The World's the Theater where she did act;
No memories, nor volumes can containe,
The nine *Olymp'ades* of her happy reigne .
Who was so good, so just, so learn'd, so wise,
From all the Kings on earth she won the prize ,
Nor say I more then duly is her due,
Mil'ions will testifie that this is true ;
She hath wip'd off th' aspersion of her Sex,
That women wisdome lack to play the Rex ,
Spaines Monarch sa's not so; nor yet his Hoast,
She taught them better manners to their cost.

The

The *Salique* Law had not in force now been,
If *France* had ever hop'd for such a Queen;
But can you Doctors now this point dispute,
She's argument enough to make you mute;
Since first the Sun did run, his ne'r runn'd race,
And earth had twice a yeare, a new old face:
Sin e time was time, and man unmanly man,
Come shew me such a Phœnix if you can;
W s ever people better rul'd then hers?
Was ever Land more happy, freed from stirs?
Did ever wealth in *Eng'and* so abound?
Her Victories in forraigne Coasts resound?
Ships more invincible then *Spaines*, her foe
She met, she sackt, she sunk his Armadoe;
Her stately Troops advanc'd to *Lisbons* wall,
Don Anthony in's right for to install,
She frankly help'd *Franks* (brave) distressed King,
The States united now her fame doe sing,
She their Protectrix was, they well doe know.
Unto our dread Virago, what they owe:
Her Nobles sacrific'd their noble bloud,
Nor men, nor coyne she spar'd, to doe them good;
The rude untamed *Irish* she did quell,
And *Tiron* bound, before her picture fell.
Had ever Prince such Counsellors as she?
Her selfe *Minerva*, caus'd them so to be;
Such Souldiers, and such Captaines never seen,
As were the subjects of our (*Pallas*) Queen:
Her Sea-men through all straights the world did round,
Terra incognita might know her found,
Her *Dryke* came laded home with *Spanish* gold,
Her *Essex* took *Cades*, their *Herculean* hold:

But

But time would faile me, so my wit would to,
To tell of halfe she did, or she could doe,
Semiramis to her is but obscure,
More infamie then fame she did procure,
She plac'd her glory but on *Babels* walls,
Worlds wonder for a time, but yet it falls,
Feirce *Tomris* (*Cyrus* Headl'm an, *Sythians* Queen)
Had put her Harnesse off, had she but seen
Our *Amazon* i'th' Camp at *Tilbery*,
(Judging all valour, and all Majesty)
Within that Princesse to have residence,
And prostrate yeelded to her Excellence.
Dido first Foundresse of proud *Carthage* walls,
(Who living consummates her Funeral)
A great *Eliza*, but compar'd with ours,
How vanisheth her glory, wealth, and powers,
Proud profuse *Cleopatra*, whose wrong name,
Instead of glory prov'd her Countries shame
Of her what worth in Story's to be seen,
But that she was a rich Ægyptian Queen,
Zenobia, potent Empresse of the East,
And of all these without compare the best,
(Whom none but great *Aurelius* could quell)
Yet for our Queen is no fit parallel:
She was a Phœnix Queen, so shall she be,
Her ashes not reviv'd more Phœnix she,
Her personall perfections, who would tell,
Must dip his Pen i'th' Heliconian Well,
Which I may not, my pride doth but aspire,
To read what others write, and then admire
Now say, have women worth, or have they none ?
Or had they some, but with our Queen ist gone ?

Nay

Nay Masculines, you have thus tax'd us long,
But she thoughdeads will vindicate our wrong.
Let such, as say our sex is void of reason,
Know 'tis a slander now, but once was treason.
But happy *England*, which had such a Queen,
O happy, happy, had those dayes still been,
But happinesse, lies in a higher sphere,
Then wonder not, *Eliza* moves not here.
Full fraught with honour, riches, and with dayes:
She set, she set, like *Titan* in his rayes,
No more shall rise or set such glorious Sun,
Untill the heavens great revolution:
If then new things, their old form must retain,
Eliza shall rule. 'then once again.

Her Epitaph.

Here sleeps T H E *Queen*, this is the royall bed
O'th' *Damask Rose*, sprung from the white and red,
Whose sweet perfume fills the all-filling aire,
This Rose is withered, once so lovely faire,
On neither tree did grow such Rose before,
The greater was our gain, our losse the more

Another.

Here lies the pride of *Queens*, pattern of *Kings*,
So blaze it fame, here's feathers for thy wings,
Here lies the envy'd, yet unparralell'd *Prince*,
Whose living vertues speak (though dead long since)
If many worlds, as that fantastick framed,
In every one, be her great glory famed.

1643   *Davids*

Davids Lamentation for *Saul,* and Jonathan, 2 Sam. 1.19.

ALas, flaine is the head of *Ifrael,*
Illuftrious *Saul,* whofe beauty did excell
Upon thy places, mountinous and high,
How did the mighty fall, and fell ing dye ?
In *Gath,* let not this thing be fpoken on,
Nor publifhed in ftreets of *Askelon,*
Left Daughters of the *Philiftins* rejoyce,
Left the uncircumcis'd lift up their voyce .
O   *Gilbo* Mounts, let never pearled dew,
Nor fruitfull fhowres your barren tops beftrew,
Nor fields of offerings e're on you grow,
Nor any pleafant thing e're may you fhow ,
For the mighty ones did foone decay,
The Shield of *Saul* was vilely caft away ,
There had his dignity fo fore a foyle,
As if his head ne're felt the facred Oyle .
Sometimes from crimfon blood of giftly flaine,
The bow of *Jonathan* ne're turn'd in vaine,
Not from the far, and fpoyles, of mighty men,
Did *Saul* with bloodleffe Sword turne back agen .

H ifun

Pleasant and lovely were they both in life,
And in their deaths was found no parting strife;
Swifter then swiftest Eagles, so were they,
Stronger then Lions, ramping for their prey.
O *Israels* Dames, o're flow your beauteous eyes,
For valiant *Saul*, who on Mount *Gilbo* lyes,
Who cloathed you in cloath of richest dye,
And choyse delights, full of variety
On your array put ornaments of gold,
Which made you yet more beauteous to behold.
O ! how in battell did the mighty fall,
In mid'st of strength not succoured at all :
O ! lovely *Ionathan*, how wert thou slaine,
In places high, full low thou dost remaine,
Distrest I am, for thee, deare *Ionathan*,
Thy love was wonderfull, passing a man,
Exceeding all the Love that's Feminine,
So pleasant hast thou been, deare brother mine
How are the mighty falne into decay,
And war-like weapons perisl ed away.

Of

Of the vanity of all worldly creatures.

AS he said vanity, so vain say I,
O vanity, O vain all under skie,
Where is the man can say, lo, I have found
On brittle earth, a consolation sound ?
What is 't in honour, to be set on high ?
No, they like beasts, and sonnes of men shall die,
And whilst they live, how oft doth turn their State ?
He's now a slave, that was a Prince of late,
What is 't in wealth, great treasures for to gain ?
No, that's but labour anxious, care and pain.
He heaps up riches, and he heaps up sorrow,
Its his to day, but who 's his heire to morrow?
What then? content in pleasures canst thou find ?
More vain then all, that's but to grasp the wind.
The senswall senses for a time they please,
Mean while the conscience rise, who shall appease ?
What is 't in beauty ? no, that's but a snare,
They'r foul enough to die, that once was fair,
What, Is 't in flowring youth or manly age ?
The first is prone to vice, the last to rage.
Where is it then ? in wisdome, learning, arts ?
Sure if on earth, it must be in those parts ,
Yet these the wisest man of men did find,
But vanity, vexation of the mind,
And he that knows the most doth still bemoan,
He knows not all, that here is to be known,
What is it then ? to doas Stoicks tell,
Nor laugh, nor weep let things go ill or well :

Such

Such stoicks are but stocks, such teaching vain:
While man is man, he shall have ease or pain.
If not in honour, beauty, age, nor treasure,
Nor yet in learning, wisdome, youth nor pleasure,
Where shall I climbe, sound, seek, search or find,
That *summum Bonum* which may stay my mind?
There is a path, no vultures eye hath seen.
Where lions fierce, nor lions whelps hath been,
Which leads unto that living Christall fount,
Who drinks thereof, the word doth naught account.
The depth, and sea, hath said its not in me,
With pearl and gold it shall not valued be:
For *Saphyre, Onix, Topas*, who will change,
Its hid from eyes of men, they count it strange,
Death and destruction, the fame hath heard,
But where, and what it is, from heaven's declar'd,
It brings to honour, which shall not decay,
It steeres with wealth, which time cann't wear away.
It yeeldeth pleasures, farre beyond conceit,
And truly beautifies without deceit.
Nor strength nor wisdome, nor fresh youth shall fade,
Nor death shall see, but are immortall made,
This pearl of price, this tree of life, this spring,
Who is possessed of, shall reign a King.
Nor change of state, nor cares shall ever see,
But wear his Crown unto eternitie,
This satiat s the soul, this stayes the mind,
The rest's but vanity, and vain we find.

FINIS.

CPSIA information can be obtained
at www.ICGtesting.com
Printed in the USA
LVHW102119030419
612909LV00011B/517/P